S0-BQC-521

America's
BLACK
&TRIBAL
COLLEGES

J. WILSON BOWMAN, Ph.D.

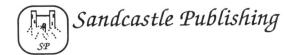
Sandcastle Publishing

America's Black and Tribal Colleges:
Copyright © 1994 by J. Wilson Bowman
Book Cover & Interior Design by Renee Rolle-Whatley

All rights reserved. No part of this book may be reproduced or transmitted in any form or by any means, electronic or mechanical, including photocopying, recording or by any informational storage or retrieval system - except by a reviewer who may quote brief passages in a review to be printed in a magazine or newspaper - without permission in writing from the author. For information contact SANDCASTLE PUBLISHING, P.O. Box 3070, South Pasadena, California 91031-6070 (213) 255-3616.

This publication is designed to provide accurate and authoritative information with regard to the subject covered. It is sold *as is*, without warranty of any kind, either express or implied, respecting the contents of this book, including but not limited to implied warranties for the book's quality, performance, merchantability, or fitness for any paricular purpose. The author assumes no responsibility for errors, inaccuracies, omissions or any other inconsistency herein. Neither the author, Sandcastle Publishing or its dealers or distributors shall be liable to the purchaser or any other person or entity with respect to any liability, loss, or damage caused or alleged to be caused directly or indirectly by this book. It is sold with the understanding that the book provides educational material and is not rendering other professional recommendations. Any slights against people or organizations are unintentional. Readers should contact the schools of their choice for complete up-to-date information on tuition fees, expenses and courses offered.

Publisher's Cataloging in Publication
(Prepared by Quality Books Inc.)

Bowman, J. Wilson
America's black and tribal colleges : the comprehensive guide to
historically & predominantly Black and American Indian colleges & universities /J. Wilson Bowman ; forewords by Marva N. Collins and Patsy A. Kruse.
p. cm.
Includes bibliographical references and index.
ISBN 1-883995-02-7

1. Afro-American universities and colleges--Guide-book. 2. Afro-American universities and colleges--History--Guide-books. 3. American Indian universities and colleges--Guide-book. 4. American Indian universities and colleges--History--Guide-books. I. Title. 5. Universities and colleges--United States. 6. Church schools--United States--History.

LC2781.B6 1994   378.73   94-66573

Printed in the United States of America

96 95 94   10 9 8 7 6 5 4 3 2 1

Dedication

To my family with love,
Kim, Chris, Miles, Cheryl, Patti and Kaela;
And most of all to Richard,
my husband,
the wind beneath my wings.

Acknowledgements

This book is intended primarily to assist the many students and their parents, counselors, and college administrators who are in search of an affordable and rewarding institution of higher learning.

My sincere thanks and appreciation go out to all the individuals, especially those at the many colleges and universities, who gave their valuable time and insights during the development of this book. The effort, I think, was worth it.

Contents

Contents

Foreword: *Why Black Colleges?*

The Age of Reason, the Age of Analysis, and the Age of Ideology represent the history of civilization. We as a people must return to the Age of Analysis. Dr. King followed the examples of Martin Buber, Thoreau, Emerson, Aristophanes, Euripides and Gandhi. It is time that students begin to study the thought of these great men; add some of their own thought, and do something with their lives. Our dilemmas are not exclusively Black ones, they are dilemmas shared by mankind. We must realize that strides made by any people have not been easy.

This must become the Age of Black College Survival. Without Black colleges, Blacks never could have made the financial and economic strides evident today. However, our people are nevertheless floating on a rising tide of mediocrity, complacency and handwringing, lamenting the difficulties of making it against such Herculean odds. We must summon the Black colleges to help us succeed. Our freedom has been bought with sweat, blood, tears, determination, curiosity, forbearance and hard work. The role of the Black college is to teach our children how to acknowledge our merits, cultivate them and succeed.

Our Black colleges have dared to accept impossible challenges—and they have found glorious things in our young. How many of our students learn for themselves, for their own betterment, rather than having assignments merely thrust upon them? Readers are leaders. Thinkers succeed. Determination and perseverance move the world; thinking that others will do it for us is a sure way to fail. Only Black colleges can say this to students without risk of being misunderstood.

Who will teach our children to read *The New York Times* bestseller list each week, to know what is going on in the world besides the latest top ten record listing; to dare to dream; to dare to aspire? Only Black colleges can dare our students to dream not only of buying that dream house with the two-car garage, but also of owning the car franchise itself.

Black colleges in the past became mentors, surrogate parents and beacons imparting light to the hopeless. Today, these colleges with the same deliberation have dared use their faculties and commitment to bring to useful fruition minds that might otherwise have been wasted. Black colleges make the impossible possible.

Most Black colleges accept our students when other institutions would not accept them, with their abysmal test scores and poor preparation. This means that these students have an obligation to work twice as hard to master those skills that they have not already been taught. They must prove that they can become scholars and contributors to the world.

It has been through my determination to succeed, that I have been able to bring pride to my people, to my college (Clark College in Atlanta) and to my family. I sought to be superior in whatever I did—not for me, but for those who must follow. I doubt if I could have felt so strongly the needs of my people without a Black college experience. I removed myself from the "Age of the Shrug" with its "so-what-it-is-not-my-problem" attitude, because this is what I was taught in a Black college.

Much has been taken from us as a people. With Black colleges much still abides. They are promoters of excellence, self-esteem, pride in race, and hope for the future. With tempered hopes and determined faith, we will emerge as a new order in society. We must maintain our legacy in Black colleges—the only chance for some, a second chance for others. *We, too, are achievers. We, too, can become excellent.* Let us pull together to maintain the vibrancy and viability of Black colleges.

— Marva N. Collins
Founder, Director Westside Preparatory School
Chicago, Illinois

Foreword: *Why Tribal Colleges?*

Indian education is thousands of years old. Prior to the time that Europeans came to the Americas, Indian people had already established schooling as an integral part of life. Today, we know that education ensures our existence as a distinct people and helps us maintain our spiritual relationship with the natural world.

Subsequent to European settlement in North America, the task of Indian teachers became increasingly difficult. Education was the tool used to push forward assimilation of the Indian people into the new Euro-American culture.

This campaign of assimilation became official in 1568 when the first formal school for North American Indians was founded by Jesuit missionaries. It was not until the 1960s that the Indian community finally establish a strong enough voice to take charge of the education of our people.

The hundreds of years before 1960 were a time of struggle. We experienced removal from our lands and elimination of the schools we had created. Towards the end of the nineteenth century, our children were shipped off to boarding schools against the wishes of their parents. If parents resisted, their food rations were withheld. Indian children were *taught* that traditional ways were wrong and that they must forget their Indian heritage. Many children ran away, some died from diseases contracted at these boarding school, and still others committed suicide.

The decade of the 1960s saw the emergence of new ways of thinking about the connection between ethnically diverse students and the culture of the classroom. The 1969 Senate report, *Indian Education: A National Tragedy—A National Challenge* concluded that the policies for educating American Indians were a failure of major proportions. While the committee made several recommendations, one in particular changed the future for Indian children. The recommendation: Indian participation and control over our own educational programs had to increase if our children were to survive. Finally, because of this report, reorganization of the Indian education program became a goal for the federal government.

In the late 1960s, the Navajo established the first tribally controlled college, Navajo Community College in Tsaile, Arizona. Over the next ten years, fifteen tribally controlled colleges were established on or near reservations. Currently, there are over twenty-four Indian controlled colleges.

The success of the tribal-based education system can now be measured by the increase in the number of students seeking and graduating from these institutions.

In 1976, the National Advisory Council on Indian Education (NACIE) stated, in part, that Indian education is a method of teaching that revives an appreciation for Indian heritage and generates a positive self image...educational policies should respect the wishes and the desires of the Indian people to design and manage their own educational programs...education programs should have full involvement of Indian parents and community members...(and) include the method and content of teaching which are designed and developed by Indian educators and Indian people reflecting Indian concepts and cultural values..(Indian education) is necessary because conventional education puts the Indian child at a disadvantage so far as learning is concerned...Indian concepts about humanity add to the more conventional emphasis on technical learning skills by putting equal emphasis on universal harmony and creating a basis for deeper appreciation for life and the universe in a spiritual context...creates in a child a positive outlook for learning new skills and knowledge...to develop the intrinsic values of an individual so that one's ability is balanced with one's appreciation and understanding.

—Patsy A. Kruse
Commissioner
Los Angeles City/County Native American Indian Commission, 1994

Introduction

Some may ask why Black colleges? Why Tribal (American Indian) colleges? My question would be - *why not?* We have single sex colleges. We have Catholic colleges. We have West Point.

Between the end of the Civil War and the beginning of World War I, several educational foundations were established specifically to advance the education of Blacks in America. By the 1900s there were nearly 30,000 schools focused on the preparation of teachers for black schools throughout the South. A serious commitment to the education of the American Indian surfaced in 1968 with the opening of Navajo Community College in Arizona.

The historically and/or predominantly black and tribal institutions have sharply focused missions. They offer some of the best bargains in higher education in the United States. Most of these small, scholarly enclaves devote themselves to undergraduates. The student/faculty ratio is usually low, averaging fifteen-to-one. The schools are not as selective as the larger more expensive schools and they are less likely to screen out promising minority students.

These specialty colleges offer small class sizes, reasonable tuition, close student/professor relationships, supervised living environments, and challenging opportunities rarely afforded minority students at majority institutions. Perhaps most important, these campuses help congregate role models and mentors. There is also no subtle discouragement, no lowered expectations.

Students are afforded the opportunities for leadership roles in student government, student newspaper, the yearbook, dramatics, recitals, concerts, art activities and athletic events provide. These organizations help students develop leadership skills and teamwork abilities.

History has shown that American Indians attending tribal colleges (TCs) and African Americans attending historically and predominantly black colleges and universities (H/PBCUs) are more likely to complete a degree than those attending predominantly non-minority institutions. The black and tribal colleges have demonstrated success in providing quality education. Without these institutions, the number of Blacks and American Indians participating in education beyond high school would be severely limited. This diverse group of institutions has provided the passage to middle-class for countless Blacks from poverty ridden areas of the rural south and inner cities and for American Indians from the Plains area.

As learning institutions, these colleges challenge and assist students to grow and become active participants in society. Most of the tribally-controlled colleges provide the first two years of higher education, though several are four year institutions and others are moving in that direction. Specifically, the tribal colleges are student-centered and promote the preservation of the customs, beliefs, language, culture and history of the American Indian.

The H/PBCUs and TCs are committed. They provide a special environment at an important time in the life of the young adult. They give the African-American and American Indian youth a sense that they are in charge and that success is attainable.

There is no doubt that these colleges and universities play an important role. Traditionally, the historically black colleges enroll less than 18% of the African-American students enrolled in higher education. Yet they account for more than 35% of the African-American college graduates. It can be inferred that the same will hold true for the tribal colleges.

I am a graduate of a historically black college, my children have attended Tuskegee, Howard, and Xavier Universities. It is without hesitation that I encourage parents to consider the benefits derived from attending schools designed to address specific ethnic considerations.

These schools have done much with very little funding and they provide the diversity that is increasingly evident throughout higher education.

My question, *why not?*

—*J. Wilson Bowman*
**Tuskegee University /
University of California, Berkeley**

Financial Aid For Education

O**pportunities** for student financial aid are available to almost every student who can show either financial need, superior academic achievement, or talent in special fields of study: i.e., art, athletics, drama, music, etc. Financial aid is also available from a combination of federal, state, local, and institutional sources.

Funds are available through the following programs:

GRANTS   -   awards that do not have to be repaid

LOANS   -   funds available to cover educational cost, which require repayment. Payment is generally required to begin nine months after leaving college, either because of graduation or withdrawal.

SCHOLARSHIPS   -   awards based upon academic achievement, and/or financial need.

The US Department of Education publishes the *Student Guide*, an annual resource explaining the process for obtaining federal aid. It gives current information regarding student eligibility requirements, financial need, deadlines, and lists borrower rights and responsibilities as well. Federal assistance is available through the following aid programs:

1. Pell Grants
2. Federal Supplemental Education Opportunity Grant (FSEOG)
3. College Work Study (CWS)
4. Perkins Loans (NDSL - National Direct Student Loan)
5. Stafford Loans (GSL - Guaranteed Student Loan)
6. Parents Loan for Undergraduate Students (PLUS)
7. Supplemental Loans for Students (SLS)

Students should seek information about all of the available funding sources *as early as possible*. The application process can be complicated. Assistance in applying for financial aid is available from college financial aid officers and from school financial publications.

The National Commission of Student Financial Assistance estimates that billions of dollars in aid from the private sector are unused each year. These dollars for scholars are available to those who are willing to devote some time and energy to the search. In Appendix G, you will find a selected list of over 100 financial aid programs geared toward minority students, though many are applicable regardless of race. It is not intended to be an exhaustive list, nor is this an endorsement of the publications listed.

The search for financial aid should start with your high school or community college counselor/financial aid officer. Next, read the newspaper. Here you will find information identifying local organizations such as alumni groups, sororities, etc. who are planning scholarship events. Contact the Chamber of Commerce for a list of the local businesses, many of which award scholarships annually. Once you have narrowed your choice for an academic institution, the serious financial aid search begins and requests for assistance from the private-sector, government and from the institution itself can be initiated.

Appendix G is divided into several broad categories: religious, professional, social, etc. Select the ones that best fit your personal profile and your academic objective. For those scholarships that appear to be the most promising, send a self-addressed, stamped envelope to the organization. Your letter should be simple and straight forward. I've included an example below:

Dear Sir/Madam:

I am a junior at _____ high school, and will be applying for admission to _____ College/ University for the fall, 19___, with a major in _____. In order to attend college, I will need financial assistance. Please send me all information necessary to apply for the financial awards program available from your organization. Enclosed you will find a self-addressed, stamped envelope. Receiving the information as soon as possible, will be much appreciated.

Thank you, in advance, for your cooperation.

Sincerely,

_____

Admission

Admission to a college is determined on an individual basis and is dependent primarily upon the student's desire, commitment and the willingness to apply himself/herself in a higher education setting.

Some schools do promote early admission. Jackson State University and Morehouse College, for example, accept eleventh grade students who have superior academic records. Academically talented students, can, with the recommendation of their principal and counselor, enroll in a limited number of college courses while still in high school. This option is available at many two and four-year institutions. If you fall into this category, take advantage of the opportunity to get a jump-start.

Applicants not meeting the basic scholarship requirements can generally be considered for admission if the student is determined and exhibits ability to do college level work. The admission policy at many colleges gives consideration to provisional applicants who exhibit the characteristics necessary for success in a college environment: commitment, motivation, intelligence, aptitude, and character despite previous scholarship records.

The following items must be submitted for admission to most colleges and universities:

1. APPLICATION
A completed application requires a high school transcript indicating completion of sixteen units which must include:
  4 years of English
  2 years of Mathematics
  2 years of Natural Science
  2 years of Social Science

Most colleges will accept GED certification in lieu of a high school diploma.

2. APPLICATION FEE

Many schools require a fee for processing admission applications. This fee is referred to as the application fee and it varies for each institution. It is expected to be submitted with the application. Some institutions accept a *fee waiver* from students who are unable to pay the fee. The waiver must be requested and documentation may be required to support the claim of financial hardship.

3. ADMISSION TESTS

Results of the Scholastic Aptitude Test (SAT) or the American College Test (ACT) are generally requested. Arrangements to take one of these tests should be made through the student's secondary school.

Foreign students may be required to submit a TOEFL (Test of English as a Foreign Language) score of 525. Transfer students under the age of twenty-one must submit ACT/SAT scores.

An overall 2.0 grade point average (GPA) is generally expected. This would included grades received from ninth through twelfth.

4. LETTERS OF RECOMMENDATION

Serious consideration is usually given to letters of recommendation from counselors, high school officials, and alumni. Some schools require an essay or interview, still others require an audition for entry into music or drama departments.

A serious highly motivated student seeking entry into college can be successful despite previous negative scholarship ratings. It is very important that students who have failed to understand the relationship between high school grades and college entrance not be shut out of the opportunity inherent in a higher education. Occasionally, even the most academically prepared student in not accepted to his/her first college choice. Therefore, in determining the best college for your abilities many factors must be considered. If you are a provisional admissions student, the available student services should figure prominently in your college choices.

Remember, your first choice school might not be available, but there is always a choice. Consequently, when considering going to college, the student should apply to at least four institutions. Applications submitted should be based upon a serious review of campus admissions materials which state the specific entry requirements and identify the students they consider the *best fit* for their particular environment.

HIGH SCHOOL COURSE PLAN

COLLEGE PREPARATION SUBJECTS	9th GRADE			10th GRADE			11th GRADE			12th GRADE		
	COURSE	FALL GRADE	SPRING GRADE	COURSE	FALL GRADE	SPRING GRADE	COURSE	FALL GRADE	SPRING GRADE	COURSE	FALL GRADE	SPRING GRADE
ENGLISH												
HISTORY												
MATHEMATICS												
SCIENCE												
LANGUAGE												
ELECTIVES												

Alabama

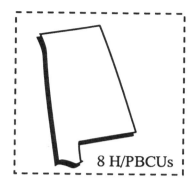

8 H/PBCUs

ALABAMA AGRICULTURAL AND MECHANICAL UNIVERSITY

Alabama A & M University started in 1875 as a junior college with two teachers and sixty-five students. William Hopper Council, an ex-slave, served as president of the college for approximately thirty-five years. The school was organized as a state normal school and became a land-grant college in 1891.

Joseph Fanning Drake took over the presidency in 1922 and the institution developed from a junior college to a four-year college offering degrees from five undergraduate schools and a school of graduate studies. From a 200-acre plot purchased in 1891, the site has expanded to encompass more than 2000 acres.

CHRONOLOGY OF NAME CHANGES

1875	-	Huntsville Normal School
1878	-	State Normal and Industrial School
1919	-	The State Agricultural and Mechanical Institute for Negroes
1948	-	Alabama Agricultural and Mechanical College
1969	-	Alabama Agricultural and Mechanical University

THE INSTITUTION

The picturesque hillside campus is composed of handsome red-brick buildings, sweeping lawns, wooded areas, drives and walk-ways. In addition there are more than 30 major buildings including an athletic complex, a Fine Arts center, a student center, 20 institutional facilities, 11 dormitories, the cafeteria and a learning resource center/library.

The college is located in Huntsville, a city with a population of approximately 170,000. Birmingham is the nearest metropolitan area.

The Address: **Alabama A & M University**
Huntsville, Alabama 35762
Telephone: (205) 851-5000
1-800-553-0816

A & M is a medium size historically Black, coeducational, state-supported land-grant college which awards the Baccalaureate and Master's degrees. It has an enrollment of approximately 4500 students and a student/faculty ratio of fourteen-to-one.

ACADEMIC PROGRAM

There are five undergraduate schools offering the Associate of Science, Bachelor of Arts, and the Bachelor of Science degrees-

- The School of Agriculture and Home Economics
- The School of Arts and Science
- The School of Business
- The School of Education
- The School of Technology

The School of Graduate Studies grants degrees in sixty-three areas, awarding the Masters of Education, Masters of Science, Masters of Business Administration, the Ed.S. and the Ph.D.

Dual-degree, reciprocal, and/or cooperative programs are available in various fields with the following institutions:

Athens State College
Georgia Institute of Technology
John C. Calhoun State Community College
Oakwood College
Tuskegee University
University of Alabama
University of Tennessee

FEES

Cost per academic year: Tuition $2400, room and board $2000.

DISTINGUISHED ALUMNI

James Turner	-	Political leader
Dr. Patricia Elzie	-	Professor of Education Albany State College
Philip Jackson	-	1982 Golf Director Dept. of Parks & Recreation Los Angeles
Dr. Herman E. Walston	-	Professor of Home Economics Kentucky State University
Dr. Earl Roberson Sr.	-	President Carver Technical College, AL

ALABAMA STATE UNIVERSITY

After beginning as a private school in 1866 for the education of Blacks, the school was chartered as a public institution in 1874. Originally located in Marion, Alabama, the school moved to Montgomery in 1887. The institution became a four-year institution in 1929. The first Baccalaureate degree was awarded in 1831.

CHRONOLOGY OF NAME CHANGES

    1874 - State Normal School and University for Colored
           Students and Teachers
    1887 - Alabama Colored Peoples University
    1889 - State Normal School for Negroes
    1946 - Alabama State College for Negroes
    1954 - Alabama State College
    1969 - Alabama State University

THE INSTITUTION

The university is an urban campus in the capital of Alabama. There are numerous shopping areas and good restaurants. Churches of various denominations are within walking distance of the University. The city has an excellent bus system, and air travel and passenger rail service is readily available.

The Address: **Alabama State University**
                  915 South Jackson Street
                  Montgomery, Alabama 36195
                  Telephone: (205) 293-4100

Alabama State is a coeducational institution. With an average enrollment of 5000 students, it has a student/faculty ratio of twenty-to-one. Students from Alabama share the friendly campus atmosphere with students from twenty-four other states and six foreign countries.

Student life at the University offers opportunities for students to participate in student government, a student newspaper, the year-book, dramatics, forensics, musical recitals and art activities. There are four chapters of national fraternities and four of national sorori-ties as well as nationally chartered professional societies and honor societies.

ACADEMIC PROGRAM

The University is divided into four degree granting divisions:
- The College of Arts and Science
- The College of Business Administration
- The College of Education
- The College of Music

The baccalaureate degree is granted in the following areas: account-ing, art/art-education, biology, business administration/education, chemistry, computer science, criminal justice, drama, economics, education, English, finance, French, health and physical education, history, human services, journalism, laboratory technology, marine science, mathematics, music, mass communication, physics, politi-cal science, psychology, sociology, Spanish and speech.

FEES

Cost per academic year: tuition, room and board $6000 to $7000.

DISTINGUISHED ALUMNI

Yvonne Kennedy, Ph.D.   -   President, Bishop Junior College, 1991-92 National President of the Delta Sigma Theta sorority

Bishop Joseph L. Howze -   Bishop of Biloxi, MS Catholic Archdiocese

MILES COLLEGE

Miles College was founded in 1905 by the Christian Methodist Episcopal Church. For the first half of the twentieth century, Miles College was the only four-year college in metropolitan Birmingham open to Black students. The first postsecondary level offering was in 1907 and the first baccalaureate degree was awarded in 1911.

CHRONOLOGY OF NAME CHANGES

    1905 - Miles Memorial College
    1911 - Miles College

THE INSTITUTION

Miles, an urban campus, is located in the western section of Birmingham on thirty-one acre site with twenty-one buildings. Transportation to and from the campus is available on the public bus transit system. Most of the major airlines service the Birmingham area. Passenger rail service is also available.

The Address: **Miles College**
                      5500 Myron Massey Blvd.
                      Fairfield, Alabama 35064
                      Telephone: (205) 923-2771
                      FAX: (205)-923-9292

Miles College is a small private coeducational institution with an average enrollment of 700 students. The student faculty ratio is about eighteen-to-one. Limited on-campus housing is available.

ACADEMIC PROGRAM

The bachelor's degree is offered in the following areas: accounting, biology, business administration, chemistry, communication, education, English, language arts, mathematics, music, political science, social science and social work.

Pre-professional programs are available in Dentistry and Medicine at the college; as well as cooperative programs in engineering and veterinary medicine with Tuskegee University; and Nursing and Allied Health with the University of Alabama.

FEES

Cost per academic year: tuition, room and board $7000.

DISTINGUISHED ALUMNI

Dr. Perry W. Ward	-	President, Lawson State Community College
Dr. Richard Arrington, Jr.	-	Mayor, Birmingham, Al
Mr. Fred Horn	-	Alabama State Senator

OAKWOOD COLLEGE

Oakwood College was established by the Seventh-Day Adventist Church on a one-thousand-one-hundred-and-eighty-five-acre site in Huntsville, Alabama in 1896. It is a private college affiliated with the General Conference of Seventh-day-Adventist.

CHRONOLOGY OF NAME CHANGES

    1896 - Oakwood Industrial School
    1904 - Oakwood Manual Training School
    1917 - Oakwood Junior College
    1944 - Oakwood College

THE INSTITUTION

The college is located in the north-central part of the state approximately 100 miles from Birmingham to the south and Chattanooga, Tennessee on the east. It is a relatively small, friendly town with an airport within ten miles of the campus.

The Address: **Oakwood College**
                      Oakwood Road
                      Huntsville, Alabama 35896
                      Telephone: (205) 726-7030

The average enrollment at the college is approximately 1200. On-campus residence halls house seventy-seven percent of the student body and the student/faculty ratio is approximately twenty-to-one.

ACADEMIC PROGRAM

The curriculum is varied offering dual-degree programs and cross-registration with several schools: dual-degree in architecture and engineering at Tuskegee University and cross-registration with Alabama A and M University, Athens State College, and the University of Alabama. A veterinary medicine program is available through the Consortium.

The associate and bachelor's degrees are awarded in the following: accounting, agricultural science, allied health fields, biochemistry, biology, business, chemistry, communications, computer science and information, economics, education, English, fine arts, food science and technology, history, home economics, horticulture, journalism, mathematics, medical technology, music, natural science, psychology, religion, social science and theology.

FEES

Cost per academic year: tuition, room and board $9000.

DISTINGUISHED ALUMNI

Dr. Benjamin F. Reaves	-	An alumnus who became Oakwood College President
Lloyd B. Mallory	-	Concert Director Lincoln University (PA)
Dr. Thelma D. Anderson	-	Chairperson, Business Dept. Albany State College
Ina M. Boon	-	Former Director, NAACP Region IV
Wintley A. Phipps	-	Pastor, Capitol Hill S.D.A. Church, Washington, D.C.

SELMA UNIVERSITY

Selma University, originally established in 1878 and affiliated with the Baptist Church, trained Colored youth for religious service. Under the leadership of Ms. A. Stone, the Women's Baptist State Convention erected the first girls' dormitory and provided access to academic training for female students in the Black Belt region.

CHRONOLOGY OF NAME CHANGES

1878	-	Selma University
1881	-	Alabama Baptist Colored University
1908	-	Selma University

THE INSTITUTION

The campus is located approximately forty-five miles west of Montgomery and within walking distance to the nearby shopping center. Proximity to Montgomery makes for easy access to and from the campus. The major transportation is by Trailway Bus and private car.

The Address:
Selma University
1501 Lapsley Street
Selma, Alabama 36701
Telephone: (205) 872-2533

Average enrollment at the college is 200 with dormitories available on a first-come first-served basis. Each student is assigned by the Academic Dean to a faculty advisor who will assist the student in registration and planning a program of study relevant to the student's career goals.

ACADEMIC PROGRAM

To qualify for the baccalaureate degree, the student must complete the general education curriculum (50 semester credit hours). The core curriculum is designed to develop values, skills and attitudes in students which will equip them to compete in today's society. The university is divided into the following academic divisions:

- Business
- Computer Science and Mathematics
- Health, Physical Education and Recreation
- Humanities and Social Sciences
- Natural Sciences
- Religion

The college offers the Bachelor of Arts in Religion and the Bachelor of Science in Biology, Business Administration and Management Information Systems. The Associate of Arts degree is also offered in a variety of fields.

FEES

Cost per academic year: tuition, room and board $5000.

DISTINGUISHED ALUMNI

Burnest Webster Dawson   -   President
                                 Selma University
Dr. T.J. Jemison   -   President
                                 National Baptist
                                 Convention

STILLMAN COLLEGE

Stillman College is a private school affiliated with the Presbyterian Church. Established in 1876 as a school to train ministers, it became a junior college in 1937 and a four-year institution in 1948. The college awarded its first baccalaureate in 1951.

CHRONOLOGY OF NAME CHANGES

1876	-	Tuscaloosa Institute
1895	-	Stillman Institute
1948	-	Stillman College

INSTITUTION

The one-hundred-acre campus is located forty-five minutes south-west of Birmingham, the largest city in the state and steel capital of the South. Proximity to Birmingham makes for ease of transportation to and from the campus.

The Address: **Stillman College**
P.O. Box Drawer 1430
Tuscaloosa, Alabama 35403
Telephone: (205) 349-4240
1-800-841-5722

The average enrollment at the college is 700 and the student/faculty ratio is fifteen-to-one. On-campus housing is available.

ACADEMIC PROGRAM

A bachelor's degree is awarded in the following areas: biology, business administration, chemistry, communications, computer science, education, engineering, English, health and physical education, history, mathematics, music, nursing, pre-dental, pre-med, psychology, physics, religion and sociology.

FEES

Cost per academic year: tuition $3000, room and board $2500.

DISTINGUISHED ALUMNI

Dr. Alex A. Chambers	-	Former President Lane College
Bryant Melton	-	Alabama State Representative
Dr. Haywood Strickland	-	Director, Grants Management, UNCF
Dr. Lenore Poe	-	Psychotherapist Berkeley, CA

TALLADEGA COLLEGE

Talladega college is a private school affiliated with the United Church of Christ. It was founded in 1867 by the American Missionary Association and originally established as a primary school. It was incorporated in 1869 and chartered in 1889. The first instruction at the postsecondary level was in 1890 and the first baccalaureate degree was awarded in 1895.

THE INSTITUTION

The 430-acre campus is situated between Atlanta (seventy-five miles east) and Birmingham (40 miles west). Talladega is accessible by bus, passenger rail service and private car.

The Address: **Talladega College**
                      627 West Battle Street
                      Talladega, Alabama 35160
                      Telephone: (205) 362-0206
                                  1-800-633-2440

Talladega has an average enrollment of approximately 750 and a student/faculty ratio of twelve-to-one. On-campus housing is available.

ACADEMIC PROGRAM

The following programs are available for selection as the major area of study: biology, business administration, chemistry, communications, computer science, economics, education, English, foreign language, history, language, mathematics, music, physical education, physics, psychology, public administration, rehabilitation services, social welfare work, and sociology.

Dual-degree programs are available in: biomedical science with Meharry Medical College, engineering with Auburn University, engineering and veterinary medicine with Tuskegee University, and pharmacy with Florida Agricultural and Mechanical University.

FEES

Cost per academic year: tuition $3500, room and board $2700.

DISTINGUISHED ALUMNI

Jewel Plummer Cobb -	Former President, California State University, Fullerton
Ruth Simm Hamilton -	Professor, Michigan State University Trustee - T I A A
Dr. William R. Harvey -	President, Hampton Univ.
Aaron Brown -	President emeritus Albany State
Margaret B. Wilson Esq. -	Asst. Attorney General Missouri
Alberta Helyn Johnson -	First African-American woman elected to public office in Wyoming.

TUSKEGEE UNIVERSITY

Tuskegee is a private, independent institution founded in 1881 by Booker T. Washington. The first instruction at the postsecondary level was offered in 1923 and the first baccalaureate degree was awarded in 1925. The founder of the United Negro College Fund (UNCF) was Dr. Frederick D. Patterson, third president of Tuskegee University.

CHRONOLOGY OF NAME CHANGES

1881 - Tuskegee Normal and Industrial Institute
1937 - Tuskegee Institute
1986 - Tuskegee University

THE INSTITUTION

Tuskegee is located 40 miles east of Montgomery, 75 miles south of Birmingham and 135 miles northeast of Atlanta. The campus is accessible by bus and car. Most students fly into either Montgomery or Atlanta and use automobile transportation to the campus.

The Address: **Tuskegee University**
Tuskegee, Alabama 36088
Telephone: (205) 727-8580

Tuskegee is one of the best known historically black colleges. It was the first black institution to be declared a National Historic Landmark and is the only "living" college campus designated a National Historic Site and District by Congress. Much of the two-hundred-acre campus was built by former slaves. The university has an average enrollment of 3000 students. On-campus residence halls house fifty-one percent of the student body and housing is available for married students. Both Army and Air Force ROTC programs thrive here. It was the first site for the training of black military pilots and has more graduates who became flag officers than any other institution. Tuskegee established the first nursing degree in Alabama. The school has a student/faculty ratio of fifteen-to-one.

ACADEMIC PROGRAM

Dual-degree programs are offered with several colleges including Bethune-Cookman College, College of the Virgin Islands, Stillman College and Rust College. A cooperative bachelor degree is offered in forestry with Auburn University, Iowa State University, N.C. State University at Raleigh, University of Michigan, Virginia Polytechnic Institute and State University.

Degrees are offered in accounting, agribusiness, aerospace science, animal science, biology, building construction, business administration, chemistry, computer science, counseling/student personnel, economics, education, engineering, English, food science and technology, history, home economics, industrial arts, mathematics, medical technology, nursing, occupational therapy, physical education, physics, plant and soil science, political science, psychology, radiology technology, social welfare work, sociology and veterinary medicine.

The strongest programs are in engineering, aerospace science and veterinary medicine.

FEES

Cost per academic semester: tuition $3400, room and board, $1700.

DISTINGUISHED ALUMNI

Ralph Waldo Ellison - Novelist, Invisible Man & other works

Chappie James - First US Four-Star General

Herman Jerome Russell - Millionaire Builder/ Land Developer

Lionel Brockman Richie - Muscian

Keenan Ivory Wayans - TV Actor/Producer

William Dawson - Internationally known Muscian/Composer/ Conductor

Arthur W. Mitchell - First Black Democrat ever elected to serve in the U.S. Congress

Dr. Billy C. Black - President, Albany State

Elizabeth E. Wright - Founder, Voorhees College

Dr. Matthew Jenkins - CEO SDD Enterprises Inc. Entrepreneur/Philanthropist

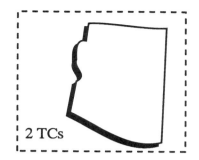

2 TCs

AMERICAN INDIAN BIBLE COLLEGE

In 1994, American Indian Bible College (AIBC) stands as the only accredited Native American Christian College in the nation. It is a regional college of the General Council of the Assemblies of God. AIBC receives no federal subsidy, as do other Indian colleges. It is sponsored by eleven districts and the Division of Home Missions. Over thirty tribes are represented on the campus including Navajo, Apache, Makah, Pima, Aleut, Chippewa, Cherokee, Pomo, Mayan, and Oneida. The college exists primarily to prepare Native Americans for a life of ministry.

THE INSTITUTION

The Address: **American Indian Bible College**
10020 North Fifteenth Avenue
Phoenix, Arizona 80521-2199
Telephone: (1-800) 933-3828

The attractive hillside campus is located in the northwest section of Phoenix and is easily accessible by the local transit system. It is close to several large shopping centers. The nearness of the business community provides a wide variety of job opportunities.

Students seeking admission must submit a favorable pastoral recommendation, an official high school diploma or GED certificate, or a recognized high school proficiency examination certificate.

ACADEMIC PROGRAM

The College offers the Associate of Arts and the Bachelor of Arts degrees.

The three bachelor programs are Ministerial Studies, Christian Education and Elementary Education. The associate degree is designed to prepare students for entry-level office positions and in management.

Students can participate in various athletic activities including basketball, golf, volleyball, bowling, and swimming. The men's and women's basketball and volleyball teams compete with other Christian colleges. AIBC is a member of the National Christian College Athletic Association (NCCAA).

FEES

Cost per academic semester: tuition $1350, room and board $1400, fees and books $400.

NAVAJO COMMUNITY COLLEGE

THE INSTITUTION

Navajo Community College is a federally funded two-year coeducational college, founded in 1968. It is located on 1200 rural acres and provides housing for 285 students.

The Address: **Navajo Community College**
Tsaile, Arizona 86556
Telephone: (602) 724-3311 ext 112

The average enrollment is 1800 students.

ACADEMIC PROGRAM

The college awards the Associate of Arts, the Associate of Science and the Associate of Applied Science. Majors offered are art, business administration, computer information systems, earth science education, engineering, health science, liberal arts/general studies, Native American Studies, psychology, secretarial studies/ office management, social studies, social work, and welding technology.

FEES

Cost per academic year: tuition $1400, room and board $3000.

3 H/PBCUs

ARKANSAS BAPTIST COLLEGE

Arkansas Baptist College is a private institution affiliated with the Arkansas Consolidated Baptist Convention. It was established in 1884. The first instruction at the baccalaureate level began near the turn of the century.

THE INSTITUTION

The college is located in Little Rock, the state capital and largest city. The city offers a fascinating blend of antebellum homes and modern metropolitan buildings. Available relatively close to the campus one can find shopping centers, restaurants and a variety of churches. Transportation to the campus is available by bus system, passenger rail service and air travel.

The Address: **Arkansas Baptist College**
1600 Bishop Street
Little Rock, Arkansas 72202
Telephone: (501) 374-7856

Arkansas Baptist is a small liberal arts college with an enrollment of less than 500 and a student/faculty ratio of sixteen-to-one. On-campus housing is available on a first-come first-served basis.

ACADEMIC PROGRAM

The college offers an interdisciplinary program in general studies and awards the baccalaureate degree in business administration, computer science, education, religion, social science and social work.

Each year, in July, the college choir performs in the Los Angeles, Detroit and New York.

FEES

Cost per academic year: tuition, room and board : $8000.

DISTINGUISHED ALUMNI

Dr. Odelle Jonas -	Vice President, Baptist Congress of Michigan
Dr. Emeral Cosby -	Principal, Persing High School Detroit
Hosea Franklin -	Associate Professor LeMoyne-Owen College

PHILANDER SMITH COLLEGE

Established as a seminary, Philander is a private, independent institution affiliated with the United Methodist Church. The first postsecondary instruction was offered in 1877. The school was chartered in 1883 and awarded the first bachelor's degree in 1888.

CHRONOLOGY OF NAME CHANGES

1877 - Walden Seminary
1882 - Philander Smith College

THE INSTITUTION

Philander Smith College is located in Little Rock which is the capital, the largest city and the geographical center of the state of Arkansas. The college's twenty-acre campus is in the heart of the downtown area. It is served by mass transit bus system, an airport eight miles from the campus and passenger rail service less than three miles from campus.

The Address: **Philander Smith College**
812 West 13th Street
Little Rock, Arkansas 72202
Telephone: (501) 375-9845

With an enrollment averaging 500, a student/faculty ratio of ten-to-one, Philander Smith College offers small, personal classes with concerned instructors. On-campus residence halls house 17 percent of the students.

ACADEMIC PROGRAM

The academic programs are divided into five basic areas:
- Business and Economics
- Education
- Humanities
- Natural and Physical Science
- Social Science

A baccalaureate degree is awarded in biology, business administration, chemistry, education, English, mass communication, health, physical education and recreation, home economics, mathematics, medical technology, philosophy and religion, political science, psychology, secretarial science, social work and sociology. Additionally, a dual-degree program in engineering with Tuskegee University is available.

FEES

Cost per academic year: tuition $2700, room and board, $2500.

DISTINGUISHED ALUMNI

Ozell Sutton	-	Past National President of Alpha Phi Alpha Fraternity
Eddie Reed, M.D.	-	Cancer Research Scientist
Lottie Shackleford	-	First Female Mayor of Little Rock, Arkansas
Leslie T. Rogers	-	Associate Professor, Rust College
Sherman E. Tate	-	Vice President, Consumer & Community Affairs, Arkansas Louisiana Gas Co.
Carl Gordon Harris	-	Department Head Norfolk State

UNIVERSITY OF ARKANSAS
AT PINE BLUFF

First instruction at the postsecondary level was offered in 1875. The first baccalaureate degree was awarded in 1882. The institute became a junior college in 1885, a senior college in 1929, and merged with University of Arkansas in 1972.

CHRONOLOGY OF NAME CHANGES

1873 - Branch Normal College
1928 - Arkansas Agricultural, Mechanical and Normal College
1972 - University of Arkansas at Pine Bluff

THE INSTITUTION

Located in southeast Arkansas, the campus is approximately thirty-five miles from Little Rock, the capital and largest city in the state. Access to the campus is easy because of the proximity to the capital. A mass transit bus system and the airport serve the needs of the campus.

The Address: **University of Arkansas, Pine Bluff**
1200 N Univesary Street
Pine Bluff, Arkansas 71601-2799
Telephone: (501) 543-8492

This nearly three-hundred-acre campus is the largest institution of higher learning in southeast Arkansas. The total campus is 754 acres, with approximately 450 acres used for agricultural research and demonstration farming.

Enrollment at the college averages 3500. On-campus housing is available.

ACADEMIC PROGRAM

Degrees are offered in accounting, agriculture, astronomy, animal science, anthropology, art/advertising, biology, business administration, business education, chemistry, child/family development, communication, community development, computer science, criminal justice, drama, economics, education, English, fire control and safety, fisher biology, food science and technology, foreign language, health and physical education, history home economics, industrial arts, mathematics, mechanics, music, nursing, personnel administration, physics, political science, psychology, social science and technical teacher training.

FEES

Cost per academic year: tuition $3000, room and board $2500.

DISTINGUISHED ALUMNI

Dr. William T. Keaton	-	President, Arkansas Baptist
Dr. Herbert Carter	-	Vice Chancellor University of California Los Angeles
Edna M. Douglas	-	Past Grand Basileus Sigma Gamma Rho Sorority
Charles Marshall	-	Professor of Business Lane College
Dr. H. Beecher Hicks Jr.	-	Senior Minister Metropolitan Baptist Church Washington, D.C.

California

1 H/PBCU
1 TC

CHARLES R. DREW UNIVERSITY
OF MEDICINE AND SCIENCE

The University is named in honor of an outstanding African-American surgeon, Charles R. Drew M.D. It was chartered in 1966 as a private nonprofit educational institution. It is the only minority-focused educational center west of the Mississippi, the only minority-focused health science institution on the west coast, and one of four minority medical schools in the United States. In 1983, the university established the College of Allied Health. The first class of Physician Assistant students received the Bachelor of Science degree in June, 1988.

THE INSTITUTION

Charles Drew is located in south-central Los Angeles. Easy access to the campus is available due to its proximity to the city of Los Angeles. Airports in Los Angeles, Long Beach and Santa Ana offer a variety of options for reaching the campus for students from out of the area. In addition to a municipal bus system that runs regularly near the campus, a newly opened metro line (Blue Line) is within two blocks of the campus.

The Address: **Charles R. Drew University**
1621 E. 120th Street
Los Angeles, California 90059
Telephone: (213) 563-5851

The private coeducational institution was created to train persons to provide care to underserved populations. In 1978, the school entered into an affiliation agreement with the University of California to provide education leading to the M.D. degree. The undergraduate medical education program began in the fall of 1981. The first two years of the Drew/UCLA program are spent at UCLA and the last two years are spent at the King/Drew Medical Center. The school enrolls a maximum of twenty-four persons per year.

ACADEMIC PROGRAM

At the university is the College of Medicine, the College of Allied Health, a learning resource center, a center for community and preventive medicine, an international health institute, a Medical Magnet high school and 17 Drew Head Start centers. There is also an extensive research center, as well as nearly 30 community programs addressing teenage pregnancy, AIDS, cancer, family planning, neuroscience, alcoholism and geriatrics.

FEES

Cost per academic semester: tuition $800.

DISTINGUISHED ALUMNI/STAFF

Dr. David Satcher - President
Meharry Medical College

D-Q UNIVERSITY

D-Q University is the only American Indian college located in California and is one of four off-reservation Indian colleges.

THE INSTITUTION

The College is located in north central California in a rural setting on County Road 31 in Yolo County. It is approximately seven miles west of Davis and six miles east of Winters.

D-Q is a private two-year educational institution established in 1971. Dedicated to the progress of indigenous people through education, D-Q became the first indigenous-controlled institution of higher learning located outside a reservation.

The Address: **D-Q University**
P.O. Box 409
Davis, California 95617
Telephone: (916) 758-0470

On-campus housing is available for full-time students on a limited first-come first-served basis. The enrollment is approximately 250.

ACADEMIC PROGRAM

D-Q University's courses are articulated for transfer to the University of California and California State Universities and colleges. A curriculum of over 185 courses, which selectively lead to an Associate of Arts or an Associate of Science degree is offered in nine academic majors:
- Appropriate Technology
- Business
- Community Development
- Computer Science
- General Agriculture
- General Education

- Indigenous Studies
- Native American Fine Arts
- Social Science

Certificate Programs include:

Academic Basic Skills, Building & Landscape Maintenance, Business Management, Certified Nursing Assistant, Computer Applications, Computer Literacy, Computerized Accounting, Computerized Office Skills, Environmental Restoration/Waste Management, Heavy Equipment Operation, Hotel/Motel Management, Medical Office Technician, and Word Processing/Office Procedures.

FEES

Cost per academic year: tuition $3700, room and board $2600.

Delaware

1 H/PBCU

DELAWARE STATE COLLEGE

Delaware State, a state-supported coeducational institution, was founded in 1891. It was started as an institution to train the Colored students of Delaware. The first instruction at the postsecondary level was in held in 1892; the first baccalaureate degree was awarded in 1893.

CHRONOLOGY OF NAME CHANGES

1891	-	State College for Colored Students
1947	-	Delaware State College

THE INSTITUTION

Delaware State College can be found in the capital city of Dover which is located in the central part of Delaware. Students have use of many modes of transportation as well as easy access to water and water sports on Delaware Bay. Transportation to and from the campus is made easy by the city bus system; also available are passenger rail service and air transportation.

The Address: **Delaware State College**
1200 North Dupoint Highway
Dover, Delaware, 19901
Telephone: (302) 736-4917

The state-supported liberal arts college is located on 400 acres near the state capitol. There is limited housing available on a first-come basis for the nearly 2500 students. The faculty/student ratio is fourteen-to-one.

ACADEMIC PROGRAM

There is a wide selection of undergraduate major fields and a variety of courses in other disciplines offered by the college. The major departments are Agriculture and Natural Resources, Airway Science, Art and Art Education, Biology, Chemistry, English, Cooperative Engineering Program, Economics and Business Administration, Education, Foreign Language, Health, Physical Education, History and Political Science, Home Economics, Mathematics, Music, Nursing, Psychology, Social Work and Sociology. A dual-degree program is available in engineering with the University of Delaware.

The college offers the associate, the bachelor's and the master's degrees.

FEES

Cost per academic year: tuition, room and board $6200.

DISTINGUISHED ALUMNI

Denise M. Gaither-Hardy - Asst. Vice President
Academic Affairs
Lincoln University (PA)
Wayne Gilchrest - U.S. Representative,
1st District, Chestertown, MD
United States Congress

2 H/PBCUs

HOWARD UNIVERSITY

Howard was founded as a private university in 1867 by an Act of the U.S. Congress. The university was named after General Otis Howard, Commissioner of the Freedmen's Bureau. The university has been coeducational as well as multiracial since its first year of operations. Howard offered its first instruction at the postsecondary level in 1867; the first baccalaureate degree was awarded in 1872.

THE INSTITUTION

The main campus of 89 acres campus sits on a hill in northwest Washington, D.C., overlooking the downtown area. Located in the nation's capital, Howard provides a stimulating learning environment. Access to the White House, Library of Congress (largest library in the world), the State Treasury, the Pentagon and other government offices are among the many resources available to students who select Howard.

The campus is served by mass transit bus and subway systems. The airport is six miles from campus and passenger rail service is two miles from campus.

The Address: **Howard University**
2400 Sixth Street, NW
Washington, D.C. 20059-0001
Telephone: (202) 806-6100
1-800-822-6363

Howard is a private, coeducational institution with an enrollment that averages 12,500 students (slightly more women than men). On-campus residences house 30 percent of the students. The student/faculty ratio is ten-to-one. The university is a level-one ranked research institution, one of only 70 such institutions in the United States.

ACADEMIC PROGRAM

The academic program is divided into schools and colleges. These are:

- College of Allied Health
- College of Dentistry

- College of Fine Arts
- College of Liberal Arts
- College of Medicine
- College of Nursing
- College of Pharmacy and Pharmaceutical Sciences

- School of Architecture
- School of Business and Public Administration
- School of Communication
- School of Education
- School of Engineering
- School of Human Ecology
- School of Social Work
- School of Theology

Advanced placement for postsecondary-level work and for extra-institutional learning (life experience) is an option with evaluation based on the ACE Military Guide, portfolio, faculty assessment and personal interviews. Student exchange programs and cross-registration are available with a wide range of institutions across the United States. The university awards the following: Baccalaureate; First Professional degree in Dentistry, Law, Medicine and Theology; Master's and Doctorate. Intercollegiate athletics are available for men and women.

FEES

Cost per academic year: tuition $7000, room and board $5000.

DISTINGUISHED ALUMNI

Patricia Roberts Harris -	U.S. Secretary of HUD and first African-American woman to be a member of the President's cabinet.
Edward W. Brooke -	First African-American Senator in the 20th Century.
Christopher Edley -	Former President/CEO UNCF
Ossie Davis -	Actor
David Dinkins -	New York City's 1st African-American Mayor
Jimmie Johnson -	Washington Redskins
Mary Frances Berry -	Former Asst. Secretary of Education U.S. Dept. of Health, Education and Welfare
Alain Locke -	1st Black Rhodes Scholar
Dr. Paul W. Smith -	President, Physicians Relations Providence Hospital, D.C.
Melvin Evans -	1st Elected Governor of the United States Virgin Islands
Joseph T. McMillan -	President Huston-Tillotson College
Trudy Haynes -	Reporter, KYN-TV

UNIVERSITY OF
THE DISTRICT OF COLUMBIA

The University is a federal institution and land-grant college comprising three separately accredited campuses: Georgia/Harvard campus, Mount Vernon Square Campus and Van Ness campus. It was established in 1976 as the result of a merger of District of Columbia Teachers College (established 1851), Federal City College (established 1966) and Washington Technical College (established 1966). The first instruction at the postsecondary level was in 1977 and the first baccalaureate degree was awarded in 1978.

THE INSTITUTION

The University of the District of Columbia (UDC) is located near the nation's capitol. It is served by mass transit, bus, an airport fifteen miles from campus, passenger rail service ten miles from campus and an extensive taxi service.

The Address: **University of the District of Columbia**
4200 Connecticut Avenue
Washington, D.C. 20008
Telephone: (202) 282-7300

The University is a coeducational, urban institution that emphasizes preparation for education professions. The enrollment averages 11,000 and there is no on-campus housing. The student/faculty ratio is twenty-to-one. Intercollegiate athletics are an option in basketball, tennis and track for both men and women.

ACADEMIC PROGRAM

Degrees are awarded in the following areas: accounting, administration and supervision, airway science, architecture, audiology, biological science, business, chemistry, communication, computer science, counseling/student personnel, criminal justice, curriculum & instruction, drama, earth science, economics, education, engineering, English, foreign language, geography, health and physical education, history, home economics, horticulture, labor studies, library science, mathematics, mental health, music, nursing, philosophy, physics, political science, print management, procurement/public contract, public policy, reading, religion, social sciences, special education, speech and language pathology, and urban planning.

FEES

Cost per academic year: tuition $3000.

DISTINGUISHED ALUMNI

Floretta Duke McKenzie	-	Former Deputy Asst. Secretary-Dept. Of Education 1982-Superintendent, D.C. Public Schools
Joyce F. Leland	-	Deputy Chief of Police Metropolitan Police Dept. Washington, D.C.
Marian Johnson-Thompson	-	Molecular Virologist

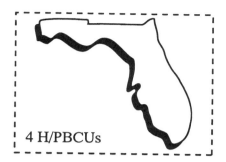

4 H/PBCUs

BETHUNE-COOKMAN COLLEGE

Bethune-Cookman college began as two separate institutions, one that started in 1872, Cookman Institute for Men, and a second in 1904, Daytona Institute for Girls. In 1923 the charter was issued and the school was established as Daytona-Cookman Collegiate Institute. The first postsecondary instruction was offered in 1932. The upper division curriculum was added in 1941 and the first baccalaureate degree was awarded in 1943. In 1931, the name of the college was changed to include "Bethune", with reference to Mary McLeod Bethune an African American educator. The college is affiliated with the United Methodist Church.

CHRONOLOGY OF NAME CHANGES

1872	-	Cookman Institute for Men
1904	-	Daytona Normal and Industrial Institute for Girls
1923	-	Daytona-Cookman Collegiate Institute
1931	-	Bethune-Cookman College

THE INSTITUTION

The college is located in Daytona Beach, one of the popular beach cities of Florida. It is approximately 200 miles east of the capital, Tallahassee, and slightly more than 200 miles north of the largest city, Miami.

The Address: **Bethune-Cookman College**
                      640 Second Avenue
                      Daytona Beach, Florida 32115
                      Telephone: (904) 255-1401
                      1-800-448-0228

Bethune-Cookman is a private, liberal arts college with an average enrollment of 2300 students and a student/faculty ratio of fifteen-to-one. The fifty-two-acre site provides housing for sixty-one percent of the student body.

ACADEMIC PROGRAM

The baccalaureate degree is granted in 35 major fields through the following divisions: business, education, humanities, science and mathematics, and social sciences. Opportunities are also available to participate in dual-degree programs with Tuskegee University, University of Florida and Florida A & M University.

FEES

Cost per academic year: tuition, room and board $8200.

DISTINGUISHED ALUMNI

Dr. Alfred S. Smith	-	Asst. VP, Ala State Univ.
Sadye Martin	-	Mayor, Plant City, FL
Rufus Young, Jr.	-	Commissioner, Daytona Beach
William Turner	-	Florida State Senator

EDWARD WATERS COLLEGE

The College was founded in 1866. It is affiliated with the African Methodist Episcopal Church and was among the first institutions specifically established to educate Blacks for the clergy. It was also the first Black institution in Florida.

CHRONOLOGY OF NAME CHANGES

1866	-	Brown Theological Institution
1874	-	Brown University
1891	-	Edward Waters College

THE INSTITUTION

The twenty-acre campus is located in Jacksonville, the third largest city in Florida. The city is less than 20 miles from the Georgia state line. Located near the mouth of the St. Johns River, Jacksonville is a great ship port and yacht harbor. The campus is served by the mass transit bus system, with the airport approximately 15 miles from campus and passenger rail service three miles from campus.

The Address:

**Edward Waters College
1658 Kings Road
Jacksonville, Florida 32209
Telephone: (904) 355-3030**

The Institution is small, private and coeducational with a fifteen-to-one student/faculty ratio.

ACADEMIC PROGRAM

Edward Waters offers a baccalaureate degree in more than 15 majors including accounting, airway science, biology, business administration, chemistry, communications, criminal justice, education, health and physical education, mathematics, philosophy, psychology, religion, and sociology. Joint programs have been established with the University of North Florida. Housing is available on a first-come first-served basis for approximately 18 percent of the student body.

FEES

Cost per academic year: tuition, room and board $7000.

DISTINGUISHED ALUMNI

Dr. Lawrence Callahan	- Founder and Manager of five interdenominational churches in Florida and the Bahamas
Dr. Frederick Harper	- Publisher, Faculty Member Howard University
William Roberts	- Attorney-at-Law Jacksonville, Florida
John Robinson	- President, Robinson's Marketing Co.

FLORIDA AGRICULTURAL AND MECHANICAL UNIVERSITY

Established as a state college for Colored students in 1887, the first instruction at the postsecondary level began in 1905. The first baccalaureate was awarded in 1910.

The doors of the college were opened with two instructors and 15 students. It was designated a land-grant institution in 1890 and became a university in 1953.

CHRONOLOGY OF NAME CHANGES

1887 - The State Normal College for Colored Students
1909 - Florida Agricultural and Mechanical College
1953 - Florida Agricultural and Mechanical University

THE INSTITUTION

The University (called FAMU) is located on the highest of seven hills in Tallahassee (population over 140,000) and approximately twenty-two miles from the Gulf of Mexico. There are more than 1000 acres of public parks and land and numerous lakes nearby. It is located eight blocks from the Capitol Complex. Bus service is available from campus to recreational areas, shopping malls, state, county and city offices. There is also an intercampus shuttle and a daily on-campus shuttle which runs during class hours.

The FAMU campus—covered by lush shrubbery, flowering plants, and massive oaks—has 108 buildings spread across 419 acres.

The Address: **Florida Agricultural and Mechanical University**
1500 Wahnish Way
Tallahassee, Florida 32307
Telephone: (904) 599-3796

Florida A & M University (FAMU), has an average student body population of 7200 and a student/faculty ratio of eighteen-to-one. On-campus housing, available for single and married students, is provided on a first-come first-served basis. There are more than 100 student organizations on campus. This includes nationally affiliated fraternities and sororities, honor societies, religious groups, Orchesis Contemporary Dance Theater, the Playmakers Guild, the FAMU Gospel Choir and the famed Marching One Hundred.

FAMU's 282-member marching band has received national television and magazine coverage and was the first band outside the Big 10 Conference to earn the Sousa Foundation's prestigious Sudler Trophy.

FAMU has been noted for its athletic facilities which include Bragg Stadium (25,000 capacity) with a field house, locker rooms, weight room and training facility; a track and field complex with an eight-lane, all weather, four-hundred-meter track; competition grade tennis courts; two outdoor pools; baseball and softball fields; and a complex that serves as headquarters for the largest women's athletic program at any historically black institution in the country.

ACADEMIC PROGRAM

The University awards the associate, the baccalaureate, the master's and the first professional (pharmacy) degrees. The major academic areas are:
- The College of Arts and Science
- The College of Education
- The College of Engineering Sciences,
  Technology and Agriculture

- The School of Allied Health
- The School of Architecture
- The School of Business and Industry (SBI)
- The School of Journalism, Media, and Graphic Arts
- The School of Nursing
- The School of Graduate Studies
- The School of Pharmacy and Pharmaceutical Sciences
- The School of General Studies which facilitates and monitors the general education of all matriculating students.
- The FAMU/FSU College of Engineering

Off-campus and joint arrangements are available in Washington, D.C., Miami and other parts of the continental United States, and with Florida State University. Students have interned in such places as England, Puerto Rico, Australia and Switzerland.

FEES

Cost per academic year: tuition, room and board $7500.

DISTINGUISHED ALUMNI

Nat "Cannon Ball" Adderley	-	Musician
Willie Galimore, Althea Gibson	-	Athletes
Frederick S. Humphries	-	8th President, FAMU
Joseph W. Hatchett	-	U.S. Circuit Judge 5th Circuit, Tallahassee, FL
Rev. Cecil Murray	-	Sr. Minister, First AME Church, Los Angeles, CA

FLORIDA MEMORIAL COLLEGE

The College was established in 1879 as Florida Baptist Institute. A merger of Florida Baptist Institute and Florida Normal and Industrial School resulted in Florida Baptist Academy. The first instruction at the postsecondary level was offered in 1918. In 1945, the first baccalaureate was awarded.

CHRONOLOGY OF NAME CHANGES

1879	-	Florida Baptist Institute for Negroes
1892	-	Florida Normal and Industrial School
1917	-	Florida Baptist Academy
1918	-	Florida Normal and Industrial Institute
1950	-	Florida Normal and Industrial Memorial College
1963	-	Florida Memorial College

INSTITUTION

The seventy-two-acre campus is located in cosmopolitan Miami, the largest city in Florida. The campus enjoys the benefits of transportation and the recreational centers associated with this resort city. Mass transit bus service is available to the recreational areas, the shopping malls and the various libraries and other municipal service areas. It is the only Black college in the southern portion of the state.

The Address: **Florida Memorial College**
15800 Northwest 42nd Avenue
Miami, Florida 33054
Telephone: (305) 625-4141

Florida Memorial is a private, coeducational college affiliated with the Baptist Church. The college has an average enrollment of 1800 students with a student/faculty ratio of thirty-to-one. On campus housing is available for approximately 70 percent of the students.

Advanced placement for postsecondary-level work completed in secondary school and for extra-institutional (life) experience is evaluated on the basis of portfolio, faculty assessments and personal interviews. Weekly chapel is a requirement.

ACADEMIC PROGRAM

The baccalaureate degree is awarded in the following areas: accounting, airway science management, biology, business management, chemistry, computer science, economics, education, English, health and physical education, mathematics, music, philosophy, physics, political science, psychology, public affairs, religion, social science, transportation management, and visual and performing arts.

FEES

Cost per academic year: tuition $8000, room and board $2700.

DISTINGUISHED ALUMNI

Nelis J. Saunders   -   Former Michigan
Legislator, 11th District

Georgia

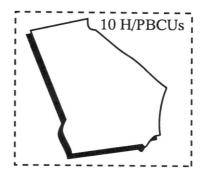

10 H/PBCUs

ALBANY STATE COLLEGE

Albany State was founded in 1903 by Joseph Wintrop Holly. The institution provided religious and manual training for Black youth of southwestern Georgia. The mission was to train teachers to teach basic academic skills and to train in the trades and industries, with special emphasis on domestic science and art. In 1932, the Board of Regents was established and the institution became part of the University System of Georgia. Albany State College is a state-supported coeducational institution.

CHRONOLOGY OF NAME CHANGES

    1903 - Albany Bible and Manual Training Institute
    1917 - Georgia Normal and Agricultural College
    1943 - Albany State College

THE INSTITUTION

The college is approximately one hundred-and-forty-five miles from Atlanta. The nearest airport is in Albany, five miles from campus. Information about the college can be obtained by writing or calling:

The Address: **Albany State College**
                 504 College Drive
                 Albany, Georgia 31705
                 Telephone: (912) 430-4600 and 430-4604

Transportation to and from the campus is available by the public bus transit system. Most of the major airlines service the Atlanta area. Passenger rail service is also available.

Albany State is a liberal arts college with an enrollment of approximately 2500 students. The student/faculty ratio is fourteen-to-one. The institution has been in a constant mode of change. In 1943 the college was granted a four-year status and was authorized to confer the bachelor's degree in elementary education and home economics. In 1954 the secondary level programs were developed for teacher preparation in science, health and physical education, business, music, mathematics, and natural science.

ACADEMIC PROGRAM

The college provides instructional programs in the following areas:

SCHOOL OF ARTS AND SCIENCES
- Department of Criminal Justice
- Department of Developmental Studies
- Department of English and Modern Languages
- Department of Fine Arts
- Department of History and Political Science
- Department of Mathematics and Computer Science
- Department of Natural Science
- Department of Psychology, Sociology, and Social Work

SCHOOL OF BUSINESS
- Department of Business Administration
- Department of Business Education and Office Administration

SCHOOL OF EDUCATION
- Department of Curriculum and Instruction
- Department of Health and Physical Education

SCHOOL OF NURSING AND ALLIED HEALTH
- Department of Nursing
- Department of Allied Health

GRADUATE SCHOOL PROGRAMS
- Department of Education
- Department of Business Administration
- Department of Criminal Justice

Albany State also offers an MBA program that allows unlimited enrollment in MBA-level courses without enrollment for a degree.

FEES

The fiscal year for the College consists of four quarters - summer, fall, winter and spring. Cost per academic quarter: tuition, room and board $2500. Students from outside the Albany area are expected to live on the campus.

DISTINGUISHED ALUMNI

Evelyn A. Hodge	-	Reading Supervisor Alabama State University
Alice Coachman Davis	-	First Black Olympics Gold Medalist, Women's Track and Field
William A. Hopkins	-	Director-Small Business Affairs, Georgia
William A. Johnson	-	Vice President, Fiscal Affairs, Albany State

THE ATLANTA CENTER

The largest cluster of private Black institutions of higher education in the world is the Atlanta University Center System (AUC). The Center is an association of seven institutions - four undergraduate colleges and three graduate institutions on adjoining campuses in the center of Atlanta.

The undergraduate schools are:
Clark Atlanta University
Morehouse College
Morris Brown College
Spelman College

The graduate schools are:
Clark Atlanta University
Morehouse College of Medicine
The Interdenominational Theological Seminary
(a federation of six Protestant seminaries)

The seven schools share a number of academic facilities and are closely linked socially. Cross-registration is enjoyed by all. Each institution remains independent, each with its own administration, board of trustees and academic specialities and each maintains its own dormitories, cafeterias and other facilities. There is a center-wide dual-degree program in engineering with Georgia Institute of Technology. The Center also sponsors career planning and place-ment where recruiters may come and interview students from the Center institutions.

Morehouse, an all-male college, and Spelman, a women's college, maintain a close academic and social relationship. The Christmas concert by the Morehouse-Spelman Glee Club is a highlight of the seasonal festivities.

The governing body of the consortium is the Atlanta University Center, Inc. Two trustees from each of the schools sit on its board along with outside members.

Located in the New South, the AUC is viewed as a preeminent location in the country for bright, talented, and successful African-Americans. It is the home to some of the most respected and well-known Black politicians and business people.

Students enrolled at AUC institutions have the opportunity to hear a world-class symphony orchestra, to view a renowned ballet company, to visit art museums and galleries, and to dine in splendid restaurants. The city is also the home of the Martin Luther King, Jr. Center for Non-Violent Social Change and the Jimmy Carter Presidential Library.

CLARK ATLANTA UNIVERSITY

Clark College was founded in 1869 by the Freedmen's Aid Society of the Methodist Episcopal Church for the purpose of providing Blacks in the South with a formal education.

The institution was organized as Clark University and chartered by the state of Georgia in 1877. The name "Clark" was given to the university in honor of Bishop Davis W. Clark, who served as the first president of the Freedmen's Aid Society and worked diligently to build institutions throughout the South to meet the educational needs of Blacks. The first baccalaureate degree was awarded in 1883. In 1988, the Boards of Trustees of Clark College and Atlanta University formally agreed to consolidate the two institutions to form a stronger, more viable institution - Clark Atlanta University.

CHRONOLOGY OF NAME CHANGES

    1869 - Clark University
    1941 - Clark College
    1989 - Clark Atlanta University

THE INSTITUTION

One mile east of the campus are the mirrored skyscrapers and modern expressways of Atlanta, the Southern metropolis. Served by taxi, bus, and MARTA (Metropolitan Atlanta Rapid Transit), the campus is easily accessible.

The Address: **Clark Atlanta University**
                    240 James P. Brawley Drive, S.W.
                    Atlanta, Georgia 30314
                    Telephone: (404) 880-8000
Enrollment at this private coeducational institution averages 2000. Clark Atlanta University is the largest of the seven member Atlanta

University Center (AUC). The college owns and operates five residence halls and a 126-unit apartment complex, Clark College Courts. With these facilities, on-campus housing is available to approximately 900 students.

ACADEMIC PROGRAM

Clark offers two degrees, the Bachelor of Arts (B.A.) and the Bachelor of Science (B.S.) Majors in the B.A. programs include accounting, art, business administration, business education, dramatic arts, economics, education, English, fashion design, history, home economics, human resources development, modern foreign language, mass communications, physical education, political science, psychology, public policy studies, restaurant and institutional management, social science and social welfare.

The B.S. is offered in the following majors: biology, chemistry, clinical dietetics, computer science, engineering (dual-degree program), mathematics, medical illustration, medical records, medical technology, medical therapy, physical therapy, physics, and pre-pharmacy and nutrition.

The college offers the dual-degree in pharmacy with Mercer University and in engineering with Georgia Technological Institute. As a result of the merger with Atlanta University, post baccalaureate options are now available at Clark Atlanta University.

FEES

Cost per academic semester: tuition, room and board $5000.

DISTINGUISHED ALUMNI

Marva Collins -	Founder and Director, Westside Preparatory School, Chicago
Marcia W. Glenn -	Lithonia, GA City Council Member

FORT VALLEY STATE COLLEGE

Fort Valley State is a four-year public institution, established initially as Fort Valley High and Industrial School in 1895. In 1939, the school merged with State Teachers and Agriculture College at Forsyth and offered the first instruction at the postsecondary level. The first baccalaureate degree was awarded in 1941.

CHRONOLOGY OF NAME CHANGES

1895 - Fort Valley High and Industrial School
1932 - Fort Valley Normal and Industrial School
1939 - Fort Valley State College

THE INSTITUTION

Atlanta, 100 miles away, is the nearest metropolitan area. The campus sits amid six-hundred-and-fifty acres of land in the heart of middle Georgia. The nearest airport is approximately twenty-eight miles from campus.

The Address: **Fort Valley State College**
805 State College Drive
Fort Valley, Georgia 31030
Telephone: (912) 825-6307

The 660-acre campus area consists of 56 buildings which are an aesthetic blending of stately brick and concrete. The college has an average enrollment of 1800 students with a student/faculty ratio of thirteen-to-one. On campus residence halls house fifty-four percent of the students. Intercollegiate athletics is available in basketball, cross-country, indoor-track, tennis, and track for men and women.

ACADEMIC PROGRAM

Majors offered are agriculture, art, computer science, criminal justice, education, engineering, English, environmental science, fashion design, home economics, language, mathematics, physical education, pre-law, political science, psychology and sociology.

Three schools comprise the academic program at Fort Valley:
* Arts and Science
* Agriculture, Home Economics, and Allied Programs
* Education, Graduate and Special Academic Programs

A dual-degree program is available with Georgia Technology.

Institutionally arranged study abroad is an available option in West Africa and through the University of Georgia at various locations, including Europe. The college is on the quarter system.

FEES

Cost per academic year: tuition $3500, room and board $2500.

DISTINGUISHED ALUMNI

Roy McKenzie	-	Executive Vice President & Co-. Founder, E.A.R. Enterprises
Dr. Cordell Wynn	-	President, Stillman College
Dr. James L. Hill	-	Dean, Albany State College

INTERDENOMINATIONAL THEOLOGICAL CENTER

The Center was founded in 1958 to address the needs for advanced theological education. It is a member of the Atlanta University Center.

THE INSTITUTION

The Interdenominational Theological Center is an ecumenical professional graduate school of theology. The constituent seminaries of the Center are Gammon Theological Seminary, Charles H. Mason Theological Seminary, Morehouse School of Religion, Phillips School of Theology, Johnson C. Smith Theological Seminary and Turner Theological Seminary. Six Protestant denominations are represented at the Center: African Methodist Episcopal, Baptist, Christian Methodist Episcopal, Presbyterian (USA), United Methodist, and Church of God in Christ.

The Address: **Interdenominational Theological Center**
671 Beckwith Street, SW
Atlanta, Georgia 30314
Telephone: (404) 522-1722

Enrollment at the Center averages 300 students seeking the first professional degree, the master's and doctorate. Dormitory accommodations as well as efficiency housing and trailers are available on a first-come first-served basis.

The student/faculty ratio is thirteen-to-one.

ACADEMIC PROGRAM

Acceptance at the college requires the bachelor's degree or its equivalent from an accredited college or university. Certification from a major official of the applicant's denomination is also required for admission to the Center.

The curriculum is organized according to four general areas of study: Biblical studies: Philosophy, Theology, Ethnics and History: Persons, Society and Culture, and the Church and its mission.

ITC offers courses leading to five degrees:
- Masters of Art in Christian Education
- Masters of Art in Church Music
- Masters of Art in Divinity
- Doctor of Ministry
- Doctor of Sacred Theology

Joint enrollment is available with Candler School of Theology of Emory University; Columbia Theological Seminary in Decatur; Erskine Theological Seminary in South Carolina.

FEES

Cost per academic year: tuition $2000, room $800, board $1200.

DISTINGUISHED ALUMNI

Willie Muse	-	Religion Instructor
		Selma University
Allen J. Sloan II	-	12th President, Miles College
Dr. Katie Cannon	-	Prof. NY Theological Seminary

MOREHOUSE COLLEGE

The college legacy goes back to Augusta, Georgia, 1867. The school, named after a white missionary, was founded in the basement of Springfield Baptist Church. The purpose was to help train newly freed slaves to read, write and prepare for the ministry and teaching.

CHRONOLOGY OF NAME CHANGES

1867	-	Augusta Institute
1879	-	Atlanta Baptist Seminary
1897	-	Atlanta Baptist College
1945	-	Morehouse College

THE INSTITUTION

Morehouse is a member of the Atlanta University Center. It is located in Atlanta, the capital and one of the great railroad and banking centers in the United States.

The Address:

Morehouse College
830 Westview Drive, S.W.
Atlanta, Georgia 30314
Telephone: (404) 681-2800 and 752-1500

It is a private independent liberal arts nonprofit college for men. The college is one of three Black four-year institutions that has a Phi Beta Kappa Chapter. It offers a dual-degree program in engineering with Georgia Institute of Technology as well as a pre-professional program in medicine, interdisciplinary programs in international studies and urban studies. With an average enrollment of 2000 students, the student/faculty ratio is twenty-to-one. On-campus housing can accommodate approximately 40 percent of the students.

ACADEMIC PROGRAM

Programs available include accounting, business administration, chemistry, child/family development, communication, computer science/information, drama theater, Earth science, economics, education, fine arts, health and physical education, mathematics, music education, natural sciences, political science and government, radio/TV and film, social science, social work, and visual and performing arts.

The Bachelor of Arts and the Bachelor of Science are the degrees awarded upon completion of an academic program.

FEES

Cost per academic year: tuition $7700, room and board $5500.

DISTINGUISHED ALUMNI

Lerone Bennett Jr.	-	Executive Editor Ebony Magazine
Samuel Dubois Cook	-	President Dillard University
Martin Luther King	-	Minister, Civil Rights Activist, Founder SCLC
Spike Lee	-	Film Maker
Samuel Nabrit	-	1st Black member of Atomic Energy Commission

MOREHOUSE SCHOOL OF MEDICINE

Morehouse College spawned a two-year medical education program in 1975. It became an independent, M.D. degree granting
institution in 1981. It was the first predominantly Black medical
school to be established in the twentieth century. The four-year
M.D. granting institution was fully accredited by the Liaison Committee on Medical Education (LCME) in 1985.

THE INSTITUTION

The Morehouse School of Medicine is located in Atlanta, Georgia.
It is a part of the Atlanta Educational Center. All modes of modern
transportation serve the city of Atlanta, the hub city for Delta
Airlines. Atlanta has more schools dedicated to providing higher
education for African-Americans than any other city in the United
States.

The Address: **Morehouse School of Medicine
720 Westview Drive, S.W.
Atlanta, Georgia 30310-1495
Telephone: (404) 752-1500**

The Morehouse School of Medicine is a member of Georgia State
University System. The private coeducational institution has an
average enrollment of one-hundred-and-thirty students. Approximately 20 students per year are recipients of the First-Professional
degree in medicine. The educational program offered by the School
of Medicine leads to the degree Doctor of Medicine (M.D.) and
focuses on scientific knowledge and meeting the primary health
care needs of underserved clients.

FEES

Cost per academic year: tuition $15,000.

DISTINGUISHED ALUMNI/STAFF

Dr. Louis Sullivan   -   Ex-President of the College, Secretary of Health and Human Services in the Cabinet of George Bush.

MORRIS BROWN COLLEGE

A private college affiliated with the African Methodist Episcopal Church, Morris Brown College was established in 1881 as an institution to educate Blacks. It offered the first instruction at the postsecondary level in 1894 and the first baccalaureate degree was awarded in 1898.

CHRONOLOGY OF NAME CHANGES

     1881- -   Morris Brown College
     1913 -   Morris Brown University
     1929 -   Morris Brown College

THE INSTITUTION

Morris Brown is a member of the Atlanta University Center.

The Address: **Morris Brown College**
                  643 Martin Luther King Jr. Dr., S.W.
                  Atlanta, Georgia 30314
                  Telephone: (404) 220-0270

The fifty-two-acre campus has an average enrollment of approximately 2000 students. On-campus residence halls house fifty percent of the students. Private housing for those who are unable to secure on-campus housing is readily available in the surrounding area.

Morris Brown has distinguished itself in the Intercollegiate National Mock Trial Competitions and Model United Nations events.

ACADEMIC PROGRAM

Majors are offered in the following areas: accounting, allied health, biology, business administration, chemistry, computer sciences, criminal justice, economics, education, fashion design/merchandising, hotel and restaurant management, mathematics, music, nursing, physical education, physical therapy, physics, political science and government, psychology, religion, social work, sociology and urban studies.

The dual-degree program in engineering with Georgia Institute of Technology is also available in addition to study abroad in Haiti, Europe, and the Dominican Republic. The student/faculty ratio is fourteen-to-one.

FEES

Cost per academic year: $12,000.

DISTINGUISHED ALUMNI

Dr. Leonard E. Dawson	-	President Voorhees College
Percy J. Vaughn Jr.	-	Dean, College of Business Administration Alabama State University
Beverly J. Harvard	-	1st Woman Deputy of Police in Atlanta Bureau of Police Service
Virgil Hall Hodges	-	Deputy Commissioner NY State Dept. Of Labor
James A. McPherson	-	Pulitzer Prize Winner (Elbow Room)

PAINE COLLEGE

Paine is a private, liberal arts, coeducational college affiliated with the United Methodist, Christian Methodist Episcopal Church and UNCF. It was established in 1882 to insure the religious education of Black youth. The first postsecondary level instruction was held in 1891; the first baccalaureate degree was awarded in 1895.

CHRONOLOGY OF NAME CHANGES

1882	-	Paine Institute
1903	-	Paine College

THE INSTITUTION

Situated between the capitals of Georgia (Atlanta) and South Carolina (Columbia), the college is right at the border of South Carolina. The proximity to two metropolitan areas adds to the options of shopping, concerts, cultural and sporting events. There is easy access to the campus, which is served by a mass transit system and two airports with one being less than ten miles from campus. The city of Augusta also offers choices of concerts and other cultural events.

The Address: **Paine College**
1235 Fifteenth Street
Augusta, Georgia 30901-9890
Telephone: (706) 821-8200
1-800-476-7703

The average campus enrollment is approximately 700 students. More than half of the students reside on campus. Cross-registration is offered with Augusta College and Clark-Atlanta University.

ACADEMIC PROGRAM

The college offers 13 programs of study, five disciplines leading to the Bachelor of Arts or Bachelor of Science degree. Degrees are awarded in the following areas: biology, business administration, chemistry, education, English, history, mass communications, mathematics, music, psychology, religion and philosophy, and sociology.

Campus life at Paine affords students the opportunity to participate in numerous clubs, academic and religious, as well as four fraternities and four sororities.

FEES

Cost per academic year: tuition $5200, room $1100, board $1700.

DISTINGUISHED ALUMNI

Frank Yerby	-	Author
Dr. Channing H. Tobias	-	United Nations Delegate
Dr. William Harris	-	President, Texas Southern University
Dr. Shirley McBay	-	First minority to serve as Dean of Student Affairs at MIT.
Dr. Morgan C. Brown	-	Dean, Bridgewater State College (MA)
Dr. Charles G. Gomillion	-	Civil Rights Activist Former Dean, Tuskegee University
Albert Murray	-	Former Asst. District Attorney, Kings County. Owner, Hillside Inn, Pocono Mountains

SAVANNAH STATE COLLEGE

The College was established and chartered as a school for Colored youth in 1890. The first instruction at the postsecondary level was in 1926. The first baccalaureate was awarded in 1930.

CHRONOLOGY OF NAME CHANGES

1890 - Georgia State Industrial College for Colored Youth
1931 - Georgia State College
1950 - Savannah State College

THE INSTITUTION

The College is in the great export city of Savannah, located on the southeastern part of Georgia, less than five miles from the South Carolina border. All modern modes of transportation are accessible to and from the campus and the students have the opportunity to participate in water sports.

The Address: **Savannah State College**
P.O Box 20449
Savannah, Georgia, 31404
Telephone: (912) 356-2186

Savannah State College is a senior college of the University System of Georgia. It has an average enrollment of 1900 students and provides housing for 70 percent of the student population. The one-hundred-and-sixty-four-acre campus with 40 buildings has a student/faculty ratio of fifteen-to-one.

ACADEMIC PROGRAM

The degrees offered include the associate, baccalaureate and the master's. The majors available are: accounting, biology science, business administration, chemical technology, communications, criminal justice/law enforcement, economics, engineering-related technology, English, environmental science, history, humanities, journalism, marine biology, mathematics, medical laboratory technology, music, park and recreation, physics, political science, public administration, recreation/leisure, secretarial science, technology, and urban planning.

FEES

Cost per academic year: tuition $3500, room $1000, board $1500.

DISTINGUISHED ALUMNI

Mayme S. Jeffries	-	Director of Assessment Edward Waters College
Mary Dawson Walters	-	1st Black to head one of Ohio States' Library Depts.
Helen M. Mayes	-	Director Emerita Albany State College

SPELMAN COLLEGE

Spelman has the distinction of being the first Black women's college established in the United States. It is one of only two Black women's colleges in the country. The private liberal arts college was established by the Baptist Church as a seminary for women. The Rockfellow family was a major supporter of the school, which was renamed in honor of Mr. Rockfellow's mother-in-law, Lucy Henry Spelman. The first instruction at the postsecondary level was in 1897 and the first baccalaureate degree was awarded in 1901.

CHRONOLOGY OF NAME CHANGES

```
1881  -  Atlanta Baptist Female Seminary
1884  -  Spelman Seminary
1924  -  Spelman College
```

THE INSTITUTION

Spelman is a member of the Atlanta University Center. The thirty-two-acre campus is next door to Atlanta's downtown. Access is available to all modern forms of transportation. The hub of Delta's airline operation is Atlanta. Mass transit bus and train systems are readily available. Students attending Spelman have available the most modern shopping malls and entertainment possible.

The Address: **Spelman College**
350 Spelman Lane
Atlanta, Georgia 30314
Telephone: (404) 681-3643

The college has an average enrollment of 2000 students. On-campus residence halls house sixty-two percent of the students. Housing is guaranteed to out-of-town freshman. The student/faculty ratio is sixteen-to-one.

ACADEMIC PROGRAM

The baccalaureate degree is awarded in over twenty majors including: arts and science, biochemistry, biophysics, biology, computer sciences, drama, economics, English, fine arts, history, languages, life science, mathematics, music, philosophy, physical education, political science, pre-medicine, psychology and religion.

The college also offers a dual-degree program in engineering with Georgia Institute of Technology. Cross-registration and cooperative academic programs through the Consortium is also an option.

FEES

Cost per academic year: tuition $8000, room and board, $1800. board.

DISTINGUISHED ALUMNI

Marian W. Edelman J.D.	-	Founder Children's Defense Fund and Former Director, Center of Law and Education at Harvard
Esther Rolle	-	Actress
Varnette Honeywood	-	Artist
Elynor Williams	-	Director, Corporate Affairs, Hanes Group, Winston Salem, N.C.
Josephine D. Davis	-	Dean, Graduate School Albany State College
Henrietta E. Turnquest J.D.	-	NY State Representative

1 H/PBCU

CHICAGO STATE UNIVERSITY

Chicago State University began in a freight car on Blue Island September 2, 1867. It was Cook County's first teacher training school. Having proved that a teacher training school could work, the Cook County Normal School opened September 21, 1870.

CHRONOLOGY OF NAME CHANGES

1870	-	Cook County Normal School
1897	-	Chicago Normal School
1913	-	Chicago Normal College
1938	-	Chicago Teacher's College
1965	-	Illinois Teachers College
1967	-	Chicago State College
1972	-	Chicago State University

THE INSTITUTION

Chicago, the great metropolis of the Midwest, is the home of Chicago State University. The university's students are surrounded by

---

many of points of interest, which include Chicago Natural History Museum, Museum of Science and Industry, Chicago Zoological Park in Brookfield Board of Trade, Prudential Building, Stock Yards and McCormick Place. Identified as having one of the greatest railway centers in the world, and located in the heart of an arterial system, Chicago's transportation system provides easy access to the university.

The Address: **Chicago State University**
                 95th Street at King Drive
                 Chicago, Illinois 60628
                 Telephone: (312) 995-2000

Enrollment averages 6000.

The 152-acre campus consists of nine buildings: Education; Business and Health Services; Harold Washington Hall; Daniel Hale Williams Science Center; Paul and Emily Douglas Library; Raymond Cook Administration; Physical Education and Athletics; Physical Plant and William H. Robinson University Center.

ACADEMIC PROGRAM

The university is organized into five colleges. All award the baccalaureate degree:
- College of Allied Health
- College of Arts and Science
- College of Business
- College of Education
- College of Nursing

Over 50 undergraduate and 26 graduate degree programs are offered through the five colleges. The university is organized into four major divisions each administered by a vice-president:
- Academic Affairs
- Administrative Affairs
- Student Affairs
- Institutional Advancement

FEES

Cost per academic year: tuition $5000.

DISTINGUISHED ALUMNI

Edward E. Gardner	-	Founder and CEO of SoftSheen Products Company
Margaret Burroughs	-	Founder/Director Emeritus DuSable Museum of African-American History
Dr. Frank Gardner	-	Board of Examiners Chicago Public Schools
Elizabeth Harris Lawson	-	Co-chair, White House Conf. On Library & Information Services, D.C. 1979
Willye White	-	Two-time Olympic Silver Medalist

Indiana

1 H/PCBU

MARTIN UNIVERSITY

Martin University, established in 1977, is a private liberal arts institution. It received accreditation as a baccalaureate granting institution in 1986. The university specializes in the advanced academic training of adults.

CHRONOLOGY OF NAME CHANGES

    1977   -   Martin Center College
    1990   -   Martin University

THE INSTITUTION

The school is located in the state capital and largest city, Indianapolis, which lies in the middle of the state. It is a commuter school with bus transportation easily accessible.

The Address: **Martin University**
                  2171 Avondale Place
                  Indianapolis, Indiana 46305
                  Telephone: (317) 543-3235

The student population which averages 900 is more than 90 percent African-American. Forty is the average age of students attending the college. The University enjoys a student/faculty ratio of ten-to-one and specializes in accommodating adult learners. The program is student-centered, with each degree individually planned to meet the educational and career goals of the student. The specific degree, i.e. Bachelor of Arts or Bachelor of Science, is determined by the student's overall plan. Two graduate degrees are offered.

ACADEMIC PROGRAM

The Martin University curriculum is offered by nine academic divisions which include:

- Division of Behavioral Sciences
- Division of Business and Management
- Division of Communication
- Division of Fine Arts
- Division of Global and Environmental Studies
- Division of Humanities
- Division of Justice and Human Rights
- Division of Religious Studies
- Division of Sciences and Mathematics

FEES

The cost to attend the University is dependent upon the number of credit hours selected; the cost per credit hour is $200.

DISTINGUISHED ALUMNI

Grace Robinson   -   Professor, Martin University

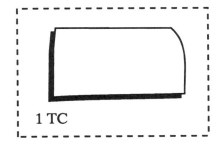

Kansas

1 TC

HASKELL INDIAN NATIONS UNIVERSITY

Haskell officially opened in 1884, under the name United States Indian Industrial Training School. The original enrollment of twenty-two Native American children increased to over 400 within one semester. The program was focused on agricultural education in grades one through five. By 1894, the school had expanded its academic training beyond eighth grade, and in 1895, the commercial department opened. It is believed that Haskell provided the first touch-typing class in the state of Kansas. In 1927, the secondary curriculum had been accredited and Haskell began offering post-high school courses. By 1935 the school began to evolve into a post-high school vocational-technical institution and from 1965 to 1970, the school operated as a vocational-technical institute. In 1970, Haskell Institute became Haskell Indian Junior College and in 1993, Haskell was approved by the North Central Association of Colleges and Schools to offer a baccalaureate program in teacher education. The name was changed at that time to Haskell Indian Nations University.

THE INSTITUTION

The 320-acre campus has more than 40 buildings and has been

designated as a Registered National Landmark. Seven modern residential halls house an average of 700 students each semester.

The Address: **Haskell Indian Nations University**
                 155 Indian Avenue
                 Lawrence, Kansas 66046
                 Telephone: (913) 749-8404

The enrollment is nearly 1000 students from 37 states and representing 163 tribes. Approximately seventy-five percent of the students live on campus.

ACADEMIC PROGRAM

The University offers the Associate of Arts, Associate of Science, Associate of Applied Sciences and the Bachelors of Science degree in Elementary Education.

The Associates of Science degree is offered with emphasis in:
- Natural Resources
  Real Property

The Associate of Applied Sciences is offered with emphasis in:
- Accounting
- Computer Information Systems
- Office Administration
- Real Property
- Maintenance Technology

The college provides a bachelor of science in education degree with a basic teaching certificate in elementary education. The program is divided into three phases of study:
- Phase one   Associate of Arts degree
- Phase two   Bachelor of Science degree
- Phase three   Teacher Certification

FEES

Haskell provides tuition free higher education to federally recognized tribal members. This is made possible by Congressional authorization in partial fulfillment of treaty and trust obligations.

Students living in residence halls receive meals at no charge. Off-campus students receive one meal per day at no charge for each day classes meet.

 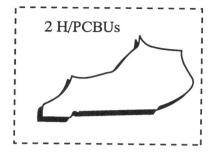

KENTUCKY STATE UNIVERSITY

Kentucky State is a state-assisted public liberal studies-oriented institution. It was established in 1886 and offered its first instruction at the postsecondary level in 1887. The first baccalaureate was awarded in 1929.

CHRONOLOGY OF NAME CHANGES

1886	-	Kentucky Normal Institute
1902	-	Kentucky Normal and Industrial Institute for Colored Persons
1926	-	Kentucky Industrial College for Colored Persons
1938	-	Kentucky State College for Negroes
1952	-	Kentucky State College
1972	-	Kentucky State University

THE INSTITUTION

The University is located in Frankfort, the capital of Kentucky, along the Kentucky River. Transportation to the campus is readily available. The city is in the northern tip of Kentucky, approximately

40 miles east of Louisville and the state of Indiana and 50 miles south of Cincinnati, Ohio. The capitol, characteristic of the stately south, houses the Kentucky Historical Society. This is also the burial site of Daniel Boone.

The Address: **Kentucky State University**
                East Main Street
                Frankfort, Kentucky, 40601
                Telephone: (502) 227-6813
                1-800-325-1716

Kentucky State has an enrollment of approximately 2500 students and offers on-campus housing on a first-come first-served basis. The student/faculty ratio is thirteen-to-one. Non-Kentucky residents, in addition to general requirements, must meet at least one of the following prerequisites: rank in the upper 40% of their high school class, score at least the national average on the SAT or demonstrate through other acceptable means the ability to pursue university academic education without substantial remedial aid.

ACADEMIC PROGRAM

Study programs are available in behavioral and social sciences, business administration, criminal justice, education, fine arts, health and physical education, home economics, humanities, industrial technology, mathematics and science, nursing and public affairs.

FEES

Cost per academic year: tuition $3200, room $1200, board $1500.

DISTINGUISHED ALUMNI

Ersa H. Poston   -   Former President, New York
Civil Services Commission

Whitney Young   -   Leader, National Urban League

Moneta Sleet Jr.   -   Photographer, Johnson Publishing
Company

Dr. Rufus Barfield   -   Vice Chancellor
University of AR (PB)

Curtis Sullivan   -   President, Omni Custom Meats, Inc.

SIMMONS UNIVERSITY BIBLE COLLEGE

Simmons University Bible College is a small private institution founded in 1897. The original mission was to train preachers and Christian educators. It is owned by the General Association of Baptist in Kentucky and offers the Bachelor of Arts and the Bachelor of Theology. The majority of students are over thirty-five and live near the college. There are no dormitory facilities.

THE INSTITUTION

The College is located in the largest and most important commercial industrial city in Kentucky. (The home of the Kentucky Derby.) There is a bus transit system, passenger rail service and access to air travel. Transportation to the campus is readily available. It is a commuter school.

The Address: **Simmons University Bible College**
1811 Dumesnil Street
Louisville, Kentucky 40210
Telephone: (502) 776-1443

FEES

The cost is $20 per credit hour and most of the students take nine credit hours per semester.

Louisiana

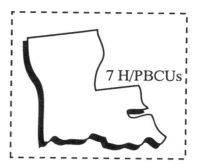

7 H/PBCUs

DILLARD UNIVERSITY

Dillard's history goes back more than a century. Straight College and New Orleans University, the parent institutions, were founded in 1869 and merged in 1930 to form one school named in honor of James Hardy Dillard, a noted scholar and educator. The University is affiliated with the United Church of Christ and the United Methodist Church. Dillard offered the first speech department in a black university and had the first accredited nursing program in the state of Louisiana.

CHRONOLOGY OF NAME CHANGES

1869	-	Straight College
1930	-	Dillard University

THE INSTITUTION

Dillard is located in Louisiana's cultural center, the beautiful city of New Orleans - home of the Mardi Gras - where the flavor is of a glamorous past, preserved in the Vieux Carre. All means of public transportation are available in the city. Part of the pleasant experience associated with attending Dillard is its location in New Orleans. The city is noted for its fine food and entertainment.

The Address: **Dillard University**
                  2601 Gentilly Boulevard
                  New Orleans, Louisiana 70122
                  Telephone: (504) 283-8822

The University is a private coeducational liberal arts undergraduate institution. It is located on a forty-six-acre tract in a lovely residential section of New Orleans. The campus consists of 19 white buildings and oak-shaded pathways and it has been called one of the prettiest colleges in the country. The enrollment is approximately 1400. Five residence halls are available and housing on campus is on a first-come first-served basis.

ACADEMIC PROGRAM

The academic program consists of six divisions of study, with majors in more than 30 areas including Japanese studies: The six divisions are:

- Division of Business
- Division of Education
- Division of Humanities
- Division of Natural Sciences
- Division of Nursing
- Division of Social Sciences

The Bachelor of Arts, Bachelor of Science and the Bachelor of Science in Nursing are conferred.

FEES

Cost per academic year: tuition, room and board $10,000.

DISTINGUISHED ALUMNI

Dr. William W. Sutton	-	President, Mississippi Valley State University
Judge Robert F. Collins	-	U.S. District Judge Eastern Division, Louisiana
Earl Lucas	-	Mayor, Mississippi's All-Black Township Mount Bayou

GRAMBLING STATE UNIVERSITY

Grambling, founded by Charles P. Adams, was established as the Colored Industrial and Agricultural school in 1901. It became a state junior college in 1928 and a four-year college in 1940. The first baccalaureate degree was awarded in 1944.

CHRONOLOGY OF NAME CHANGES

1901	-	Colored Industrial and Agricultural School
1905	-	North Louisiana Agricultural and Industrial Institute
1918	-	Lincoln Parrish Training School
1928	-	Louisiana Negro Normal and Industrial Institute
1947	-	Grambling College
1974	-	Grambling State University

THE INSTITUTION

Grambling is located in the northern part of Louisiana, sixty-five miles from the nearest metropolitan area, Shreveport, which is the third largest city in Louisiana. The airport is 40 miles from campus and public transportation provides easy access to the campus.

The Address: **Grambling State University**
Post Office Box 605
Grambling, Louisiana 71245
Telephone: (318) 247-3811

The university is a public-supported coeducational institution with an enrollment of 7000 students. There are fifty-six buildings on 240 acres. Residence halls house 67 percent of the students. The student/faculty ratio is twenty-to-one.

ACADEMIC PROGRAM

The degree granting academic units are Colleges of Liberal Arts, Science and Technology, Education, and the School of Nursing, Social Work and the Graduate Division.

The baccalaureate degree is offered in biological science, business administration, communications, computer and information sciences, education, engineering, fine and applied arts, health professions, mathematics, physical sciences, psychology, public affairs and service, and social sciences.

The master's degree is conferred in liberal studies, education, business administration, social work, criminal justice, and public administration. The doctoral degree is offered in Developmental Education.

A dual-degree program in engineering and cross-registration is offered with Louisiana Technical University. Study abroad is available in Mexico and South America.

FEES

Cost per academic year: tuition $6500, room and board $3400.

DISTINGUISHED ALUMNI

Joseph B. Johnson	-	President of Talladega
Judy Ann Mason	-	Television Script Writer
Willie Davis	-	Professional Football Player Green Bay Packers
Doug Williams	-	Professional Football Player Washington Redskins
James Harris	-	Professional Football Player Los Angeles Rams

SOUTHERN UNIVERSITY

Southern University is more than a single university. It is a system. Following along the Red River from Shreveport to Baton Rouge to New Orleans are the institutions that are part of the System. The Southern University System is the only predominantly black public university System in the nation. With its three major campuses, it covers a total campus area of 1000 acres and has more than 20,000 students.

The Baton Rouge campus was the first of the System institutions to be established. It is the oldest and the largest and the only one that offers post-baccalaureate degrees. Baton Rouge, the capital city of Louisiana, a characterized by winding drives, scenic lakes, bayous and antebellum homes. With this setting as a surrounding, the campus presents a very impressive environment. The campus was chartered as Southern University in New Orleans in 1880 and became a land-grant institution in 1892. The name, Baton Rouge, was adopted in 1914.

The New Orleans campus is primarily a commuter campus serving the greater New Orleans area. It has no dormitories.

Shreveport, the two-year campus, located in the northeast corner of the state, is a part of the third largest city in Louisiana.

The Law School is located on the Baton Rouge campus and has an administration separate from the Baton Rouge Campus. It is the newest member of the System.

THE INSTITUTION

System Office is located in Baton Rouge: **(504) 771-4680**

The members of the Southern University System are:

Southern University - New Orleans
6400 Press Drive
New Orleans, Louisiana 70126
Telephone: (504) 286-5000

Southern University - Baton Rouge
P.O. Box 9614
Southern Branch Post Office
Baton Rouge, Louisiana 70813
Telephone: (504) 711-5020

Southern University Law Center (SULA)
Lenoir Hall
Baton Rouge, Louisiana 70813
Telephone: (504) 771-5020

Southern University - Shreveport
MLK Drive
Shreveport, Louisiana 71107
Telephone (318) 674-3300

Spread out in a relatively straight line from Shreveport to New Orleans, the Southern University System provides most of the options for academic majors available in a large institution.
If one is interested in attending one of the system institutions, write directly to the campus of your choice for information.

ACADEMIC PROGRAM

With the exception of the Law School, all of the campuses offer the baccalaureate degree in accounting, art, biology, business administration, chemistry, computer science, physics, psychology, sociology and speech.

Unique to a particular campus are the following:

- Baton Rouge campus—agriculture, architecture, computer science, drama, education, engineering, geography, microbiology, music, nursing, and rehabilitation counseling.
- New Orleans campus - medical technology and zoology.

FEES

Cost per academic year: tuition, room and board $6000.

DISTINGUISHED ALUMNI

Dolores R. Spiles	-	President, Southern Univ. System
Willie Davenport	-	1968 Olympic Gold-Medalist
Clarence Williams	-	Performing Artist
Norward J. Brooks	-	Seattle City Comptroller
William J. Jefferson	-	Louisiana's first Black Congressman

XAVIER UNIVERSITY OF LOUISIANA

Xavier University of Louisiana is the only historically Black Ro-
man Catholic University in the South. The Sisters of the Blessed
Sacrament with Katharine Drexel founded the school in 1925 to
provide an affordable college education to Black and Indian Catholic youth.

CHRONOLOGY

1915	-	Established as a secondary school
1918	-	Chartered
1925	-	Became a 4-year college
1928	-	Awarded first baccalaureate degree
1933	-	Added the master's program

THE INSTITUTION

The twenty-seven-acre campus is located only minutes from the
heart of New Orleans. It is served by the mass transit system, an
airport eight miles from campus and passenger rail less than two
miles from campus.

The Address: **Xavier University**
7325 Palmetto and Pine Streets
New Orleans, Louisiana 70125
Telephone: (504) 486-7411

Xavier is a private coeducational institution. The 3400 students
enrolled represent some forty-five states and twenty foreign countries. On-campus residence halls house 25 percent of the students.
The student/faculty ratio is fifteen-to-one.

ACADEMIC PROGRAM

The Xavier curriculum is liberal arts oriented, with all students
required to take a core of prescribed courses which include theology
and philosophy.

It is recognized as a national leader in the field of minority science education and is one of only eleven schools nationwide which offers the Pharm. D. degree. Twenty-five percent of all African-American pharmacists in the US are graduates of Xavier.

The campus is ruled by the natural sciences, the area in which over 50 percent of its students major. The baccalaureate is awarded in accounting, biology, business, chemistry, communication, computer science, economics, education, engineering, English, health and physical education, history, marketing, mathematics, microbiology, music, pharmacology, philosophy, physics, political science, pre-law, psychology, social science, speech pathology, statistics, and theology.

The graduate school offers five degrees: Master of Arts, Masters of Arts in Teaching, Theology and Science, and Doctor of Pharmacy.

FEES

Cost per academic year: tuition $6000, room and board $3400.

DISTINGUISHED ALUMNI

George McKenna	-	Superintendent of Schools Inglewood, California
Alexis Herman	-	Democratic National Committee Chief-of-Staff; Named one of the 100 top outstanding business women in the U.S.
Norman C. Francis	-	Alumnus President of Xavier
Brenda August	-	Decennial Specialist U.S. Dept. of Commerce
Andolyn V. Brown	-	Vice President, Student Affairs, Wilberforce University
Dr. Milton Gordon	-	Pres. California State University, Fullerton, CA

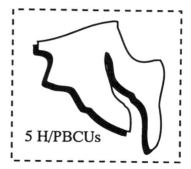

5 H/PBCUs

BOWIE STATE COLLEGE

Bowie was started in the basement of the African Methodist Church in Baltimore in 1865. It was originally established as an Industrial School for Colored Youth. The first instruction at the postsecondary level was offered in 1893. The first baccalaureate degree was awarded in 1912.

CHRONOLOGY OF NAME CHANGES

1865	-	Industrial School for Colored Youth
1908	-	Normal School No. 3
1912	-	Bowie Normal and Industrial School
1925	-	Maryland State Teachers College
1963	-	Bowie State College

THE INSTITUTION

The location of Bowie State is described as being "at the center of a triangle" formed by the nation's capital (Washington, D.C.), Annapolis, and Baltimore, MD. The university is situated in the suburbs of Pricce George County. The natural boundary of trees and forests gives the university a country-like setting.

The Washington Metropolitan Area Transit Authority (METRO), a passenger rail system and air transportation is available to serve the Bowie campus.

The Address: **Bowie State College**
Jericho Park Road
Bowie, Maryland 20715-9465
Telephone: (301) 464-6572

The campus has a total of 17 buildings on 267 acres. Tremendous growth occurred during the 1970s with the construction of the Communication Arts Center, the administration building, the physical education complex, a new library and a six-story residence hall.

On-campus housing is available for 600 students. The residence halls-Harriet Tubman, Lucretia Kennard, Dwight Holmes and the Towers, are situated on the south end of the campus. A new Honors Residence Hall houses 30 students. The university has a multicultural, multi-racial faculty, 60 percent of whom hold the doctoral degree. The student/faculty ratio is fifteen-to-one.

Bowie State is a NCAA Division II school. Students may participate in many types of sports: football, women's volleyball, men's and women's basketball, co-educational track and field softball, baseball, and co-educational tennis. The school offers sports scholarships.

In addition to the opportunities to participate in team sports, at Bowie more than 40 different activities are available for the students. These include sororities and fraternities, academic clubs, pre-professional organizations, musical organizations and drama clubs to list a few. With an average enrollment of 3000 students, eighty-five percent are from Maryland, the remaining 15 percent from several other states and 40 foreign countries.

ACADEMIC PROGRAM

Students can select from twenty-seven major fields of study. These majors, grouped by department, are:

- Behavioral Sciences and Human Services
- Business, Economics, Public Administration
- Communications
- Education and Physical Education
- History, Politics, and International Studies
- Humanities and Fine Arts
- Natural Sciences, Mathematics, and Computer Science
- Nursing
- Military Science

These departments are divided into four major area:

- Humanities
- Social Science
- Mathematics/Science
- Education/Physical Ed.

The university offers dual programs in dentistry and engineering with the University of Maryland.

Two undergraduate degrees are awarded: Bachelor of Science and Bachelor of Arts.

The graduate school grants the Masters of Education, the Masters of Arts and the Master of Science.

FEES

Cost per academic year: tuition, room and board $8000.

DISTINGUISHED ALUMNI

Lula M. Loynes	-	Subcontracts Administrator Lockheed Engr. & Mgnt. Services
John A. Austin	-	Professor, Norfolk State Univ.
Kevin L. Jefferson	-	National Minority Affairs Coordinator for Handgun Control

COPPIN STATE COLLEGE

The college was named for Fanny Jackson Coppin, who was born a slave in the District of Columbia in 1837. She was one of the first Black women to earn a degree from a major U.S. college. Coppin State College was established as a postsecondary institution offering teacher training in 1900. Initially housed in Douglass High School, it became a four-year college in 1930. The first baccalaureate degree was awarded in 1942 and in 1950 it became part of the Maryland Educational System.

CHRONOLOGY OF NAME CHANGES

1900	-	Douglass High School
1926	-	Fannie Jackson Coppin Normal School
1930	-	Coppin Teachers College
1950	-	Copin State Teachers College
1967	-	Coppin State College

THE INSTITUTION

Coppin is very much a part of Baltimore, the largest city in Maryland. The tree-lined campus occupies 38 acres in west Baltimore and is one of the city's most impressive settings for learning. It is an urban campus with easy access to public transportation. The Metro stops at Mondawin Mall, a five minute walk from campus. The proximity to the national capital makes Baltimore a city with rich heritage. Just outside the city, on a point reaching into the harbor, is the site of major bombardment during the War of 1812, which inspired Francis Scott Key to write the "Star Spangled Banner".

The Address:　**Coppin State College**
2500 West North Avenue
Baltimore, Maryland 21216
Telephone: (301) 333-5990

Enrollment varies but generally services 2300 to 3000 students. The majority of the students are from the Baltimore/District of Columbia area. Intercollegiate athletics for men and women are available. There is no on-campus housing. The student/faculty ratio is fifteen-to-one. There are more than 40 clubs and organizations available for student participation.

ACADEMIC PROGRAM

Dual-degree options are available with the Maryland State Colleges; including engineering, chemistry, general science, pre-dental, pre-pharmacy, and theology with University of Maryland. The college is divided into three major undergraduate divisions. These are:
- Division of Arts and Science
- Division of Nursing
- Division of Education

The Graduate program awards degrees in the following:
- Adult and Continuing Education
- Criminal Justice
- Correctional Education
- Rehabilitation Counseling
- Special Education

FEES

Cost per academic year: tuition $4000.

DISTINGUISHED ALUMNI

Milton Burk Allen   -   Chief Prosecutor, Maryland State Attorney for Baltimore

MORGAN STATE UNIVERSITY

Morgan State University was chartered as Centenary Bible Institution and offered first instruction at postsecondary level in 1867. The first baccalaureate degree was offered in 1895.

CHRONOLOGY OF NAME CHANGES

1867	-	Centenary Bible Institute
1890	-	Morgan College
1939	-	Morgan State College
1975	-	Morgan State University

THE INSTITUTION

Located in the northeast section of Baltimore, Maryland's largest city, students have access to a mass transit bus system, passenger rail and airport facilities. Easily accessible by car or by public transportation, the campus enjoys a residential setting with a suburban feeling. Proximity to the national capital makes this college an interesting choice.

The Address: **Morgan State University**
Cold Spring Lane
Baltimore, Maryland 21239
Telephone: (301) 444-3300

Morgan is a public co-educational institution located on 130 acres with an enrollment of 4500 students. The student/faculty ratio is sixteen-to-one.

ACADEMIC PROGRAM

Available for students is the option to participate in a variety of cooperative programs including the dual-degree in engineering with University of Pennsylvania and University of Rochester; physical therapy with University of Maryland. Cross-registration is available with Bowie State College, College of Notre Dame, Coppin State College, Goucher College, John Hopkins University, Salisbury State College, University of Baltimore and the University of Maryland. The college is divided into four divisions:

- College of Arts and Science
- School of Business Management
- School of Education and Urban
- School of Engineering

Majors are offered in accounting, architecture, art/advertising, biology, chemistry, communications, computer science, drama/theater, ecology, education, engineering, health/physical education, home economics, human services, medical technology, military science, philosophy, physics, political science, psychology, religion, social welfare work and speech.

FEES

Cost per academic year: $4500, room and board: $4500.

DISTINGUISHED ALUMNI

Earl Graves	-	Publisher, Black Enterprise
Wilson W. Goode	-	Mayor, Philadelphia
Parren J. Mitchell	-	Former U.S. Congressman
Hilda L. Joyce	-	Asst. Professor University of Virgin Islands
Willie Lanier	-	Professional Football Player Kansas City Chiefs
Frederick Oliver Boone	-	Pilot, Delta Airlines

SOJOURNER-DOUGLASS COLLEGE

Sojourner-Douglass was founded and chartered in 1972 as an affiliate to Antioch University, Ohio. It became an independent institution under Maryland law in 1980. The College is a unique, community-controlled private institution offering an educational alternative for working adults. It provides an opportunity for adult learners to study on a full-time basis by providing evening and weekend classes. The name was selected to honor the historical contributions of two Black abolitionist–Sojourner Truth and Frederick Douglass.

CHRONOLOGY OF NAME CHANGES

1972 - Homestead-Montibello College
1980 - Sojourner-Douglass College

THE INSTITUTION

The address: **Sojourner Douglass College**
500 North Caroline Street
Baltimore, Maryland, 21205
Telephone: (301) 276-0306

Sojourner is a small unique community controlled private institution. Its major focus is to provide opportunities for adult learners to study on a full-time basis by providing evening and weekend classes. The average enrollment is 400 students per year.

ACADEMIC PROGRAM

Sojourner operates on a trimester system (3 terms - 15 weeks each) system and awards the Bachelor of Arts degree. Credit for prior learning is available and students are allowed to work at their own pace.

A student may design a career speciality in any combination of the three major areas:

Administration:
- Administration and Management
- Public Administration
- Hospitality Management
- Information Systems Administration
- Business Admin.
- Health Care Admin
- Cable TV Admin.

Human and Social Resources areas:
- Criminal Justice
- Community Development
- Social Welfare/Counseling
- Gerontology
- Social Work

Human Growth and Development:
- Early Childhood Education
- Psychology

FEES

Cost per academic trimester: tuition $1600.

DISTINGUISHED ALUMNI

Hattie N. Harrison	-	Member, House of Delegates, Baltimore, 1st Black woman to chair a legislative committee
Nathan C. Irby	-	Member of the Senate, Baltimore
Betty Deacon	-	Chief of Staff Baltimore City Council

UNIVERSITY OF MARYLAND
EASTERN SHORE

The university is a coeducational institution established in 1886.

CHRONOLOGY OF NAME CHANGES

1886 - Princess Anne of the Delaware Conference
1948 - Maryland State College
1970 - University of Maryland - Eastern Shore

THE INSTITUTION

The six-hundred-acre campus is located in the southeast corner of Maryland approximately half-way between the states of Delaware and Virginia. It is a college town and the majority of the population is involved in the institution. Baltimore and D.C. are approximately 130 miles from campus.

The Address: **University of Maryland (E.S.)**
                 Princess Anne, Maryland 21853
                 Telephone: (301) 651-2200

The university is a coeducational institution with an enrollment of 1500. On-campus housing can accommodate fifty-five percent of the students. The student/faculty ratio is fifteen-to-one.

ACADEMIC PROGRAM

Degrees are offered in accounting, agriculture, airway science, allied health fields, art/advertisement, biology, building construction, business administration, chemistry, communication, computer science, counseling/student personnel, curriculum and instruction, ecology, economics, education, engineering, English, history, home economics, hotel and restaurant management, industrial arts, mathematics, music, physical education, physical therapy, and the social sciences.

FEES

Cost per academic year: tuition $4000, room: $2000, board $1500.

DISTINGUISHED ALUMNI

Ambrose Jearld, Jr.	-	Chief Research Planner
		National Marine Fisheries Service
		U.S. Department. of Commerce
Emmet H. Paige, Jr.	-	U. S. Army General
Martin J. Lamkin	-	Music Instructor
		University of Virgin Islands

1 H/PBCU
1 TC

BAY MILLS COMMUNITY COLLEGE

Bay Mills Community College is Michigan's only tribally controlled higher education institution. The building blocks for this
tribal college grew from a vocational program funded by the Department Of Education in 1981. The purpose of the original program
was to train eleven students each year for tribal employment. The
program's success resulted in the Bay Mills Tribe chartering the Bay
Mills Community College in 1984. Since that time, the college has
offered extension classes on every reservation in Michigan and in
many of their neighboring communities.

THE INSTITUTION

The library building of BMCC houses the Cultural Heritage Center.
The Center includes prehistoric and historic materials related to the
many cultures of Native North America.

The Address: **Bay Mills Community College**
Route I, P.O. Box 315 A
Brimley, Michigan 49715
Telephone: (906) 248-3365 or (906) 248-5580

Enrollment is approximately 200 students.

ACADEMIC PROGRAM

The curriculum offers certificate and associate degree programs that can be completed in one and two years.

Degrees are awarded as follows:
- Associate of Arts
  - Native American Studies
  - Social Science

- Associate of Applied Science
  - Computer Information Systems
  - Office Technology
  - Tribal Administration

- Certificate of Business
  - General Business
  - General Office
  - Retailing

Preparatory Program in Health Science
- Certification of Nursing
- Certification in Health Technician

FEES

Cost per academic semester: tuition $750.

MARYGROVE COLLEGE

Marygrove College was established in 1845 by the Sisters Servants of the Immaculate Heart of Mary. It was originally a Catholic women's college under the leadership of Theresa Maxis, a woman of color from Haiti. The college, dedicated to assisting women in developing personal values, started with approximately 300 students. Over the years the mission of the college has changed and it is currently a private coeducational liberal arts college.

CHRONOLOGY OF NAME CHANGES

    1845 -   St. Mary Academy
    1925 -   St. Mary College
    1927 -   Marygrove College

THE INSTITUTION

The campus is located on an sixty-eight-acre tract in northwest Detroit - the "Motor Capital of the World". There is excellent transportation by bus, passenger rail and air.

The Address: **Marygrove College**
                 8425 W. McNichols Road
                 Detroit, Michigan 48221
                 Telephone: (313) 862-8000

Marygrove College is an independent Catholic liberal arts college. The metropolitan campus offers dormitory accommodations for 50 percent of the approximate 1200 students on a first-come first-served basis.

ACADEMIC PROGRAM

The first-year seminar is an introduction to college life and assists students in developing academic and personal success in life. It is recommended for all beginning students.

The degrees offered include the baccalaureate and the master's as well as the Associate in Arts and the Associate in Science. Degree programs are offered in accounting, allied health, arts, biology, business, chemistry, child development, communications, computer science, correctional science, dance, English, fashion merchandising, food and nutrition, history, human ecology, mathematics, music, performing arts, physical science, political science, psychology, religion, special education, social science and sociology. The school curriculum also includes courses leading to pre-dental, pre-medicine and pre-law degrees.

FEES

Cost per academic semester: tuition $3500, private room and board $2000.

 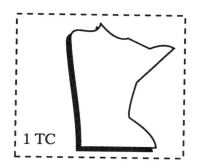

FOND DU LAC COMMUNITY COLLEGE

Fond Du Lac Community College was created by the Minnesota Legislature in 1987 and chartered as a tribal college by the Fond Du Lac Reservation that same year. The college is the product of extensive consultation among tribal and civic leaders, area business people, other concerned citizens and students.

THE INSTITUTION

Located approximately twenty minutes from Duluth, FDLCC is easily accessible from interstate 35 on a beautiful wooded 40-acre site.

The Address: **Fond Du Lac Community College**
2101 - 14th Street
Cloquet, Minnesota 55720
Telephone: (218) 879-0800

The college can accommodate 500 students.

ACADEMIC PROGRAM

The instructional program is organized into six academic areas.

DIVISION OF BUSINESS
Accounting
Business Administration and Office Administration
Marketing and Management
Office Technology

DIVISION OF CREATIVE AND COMMUNICATIVE ARTS
Art
Mass Communications
Speech
English
Music
Theatre

DIVISION OF EDUCATION
Elementary Education
Industrial Education
Physical Education
Home Economics
Ojibwe Specialist
Secondary Education

DIVISION OF MEDICINE AND ALLIED HEALTH
Dentistry
Mortuary Science
Occupational Therapy
Pharmacy
Veterinary Medicine
Medical Technology
Nursing
Optometry
Physical Therapy

DIVISION OF SCIENCE AND ENGINEERING
Agriculture
Architecture
Chemistry/Chemical Engineering
Computer Science
Forestry
Mathematics
Airway Science
Biology

Engineering
Industrial Technology
Physics

DIVISION OF SOCIAL AND BEHAVIORAL SCIENCES
Criminal Justice
History
Law
Political Science
Social Work
Geography
Human Services
Law Enforcement
Psychology
Sociology

The College offers the Associate in Arts, Associate in Science, Associate in Applied Science and the Occupational Certificate. FDLCC is designed to provide transfer-oriented curriculum paralleling the first two years of a baccalaureate degree program. For those not intending to continue their education at the four-year level, the general studies program is offered. Occupational training and continuing education for adults is also available.

FEES

Cost for full-time students per quarter: tuition $1360.

5 H/PBCUs

ALCORN STATE UNIVERSITY

Alcorn State University was established in 1871 on the site of a closed Presbyterian school for boys. It is the oldest predominantly Black land-grant institution in the United States. Located on the campus is the Oakland Memorial Chapel recognized as a nationally historic site and the location of the conferring of the first degree in the state of Mississippi.

CHRONOLOGY OF NAME CHANGES

    1871 - Alcorn University
    1878 - Alcorn Agriculture and Mechanical College
    1974 - Alcorn State University

THE INSTITUTION

Alcorn is equidistant from Vicksburg to the north and Natchez to the south, and 80 miles from Jackson. It is served by an airport 35 miles from campus and by passenger rail 90 miles away. The campus is situated in Lorman, Mississippi; surrounded with the ruins of beautiful Windsor Castle and the gigantic Mississippi river. These sites blend well with the school's century-old buildings and moss-draped trees, together creating a beautiful historic setting.

The Address: **Alcorn State University**
P.O. Box 300
Lorman, Mississippi 39096
Telephone: (601) 877-6100

Alcorn is a coeducational college with an enrollment about 3000 and a student/faculty ratio of fifteen-to-one. Most of the students live on campus in beautiful modern air-conditioned dormitories. The campus is composed of 105 buildings some of which have been designated national monuments.

ACADEMIC PROGRAM

The University awards the Bachelor of Science, Bachelor of Arts and the Bachelor of Music through the following divisions:
- Division of Arts and Sciences
- Division of Education and Psychology
- Division of Agriculture and Applied Science
- Division of Business and Economics
- Division of Nursing
- Division of General College for Excellence

The Division of Graduate Studies awards the Master of Science in Education and Master of Science in Agriculture.

FEES

Cost per academic semester: tuition, room and board $5000.

DISTINGUISHED ALUMNI

Del Anderson   -   President, San Jose City College (CA)
Alex Haley   -   Author of Roots

JACKSON STATE UNIVERSITY

Established by American Baptist Home Mission Society in 1877, the school was designed to provide training for Black youth. It is the fourth largest state-supported university in Mississippi. The first instruction at the postsecondary level was offered in 1921, and the first baccalaureate degree was awarded in 1924. In 1940, the State of Mississippi assumed control of the institution.

CHRONOLOGY OF NAME CHANGES

1877	-	Natchez Seminary
1899	-	Jackson College
1940	-	Mississippi Negro Training School
1944	-	Jackson College for Negro Teachers
1956	-	Jackson State College
1974	-	Jackson State University

THE INSTITUTION

The college is located in Jackson, the capital and largest metropolitan area in Mississippi. Transportation to and from the campus is available by mass transit bus system. An airport is eight miles away and passenger rail service is two miles from campus.

The Address: **Jackson State University**
1400 John R. Lynch Street
Jackson, Mississippi 39217
Telephone: (601) 968-2100
1-800-848-6817

Jackson is a state-supported institution with an average enrollment of 6500. On-campus housing is provided for thirty-two percent of the students. The ratio of students to faculty is twenty-one-to-one.

The bachelor's, master's and doctorate degrees are awarded for those who successfully complete prescribed curricula. The academic program is provided through:

- The School of Liberal Studies
- The School of Business
- The School of Education
- The School of Science and Technology
- The Graduate School

One hundred ninety-two degrees are offered: 51 Bachelors, 34 Masters, 105 Specialist in Education and 2 Doctoral degrees. The programs available include accounting, art biology, business administration, communication, computer science, criminal justice, ecology, economics, education, English, guidance, health and physical education, industrial administration, industrial arts, management, marine science, mathematics, microbiology, music, physics, political science, psychology, reading education, social science, sociology, speech and urban affairs.

FEES

Cost per academic year: tuition $3000, room $1500, board $1,200.

DISTINGUISHED ALUMNI

J. Paul Brownridge	-	City Treasure, Los Angeles
Walter Payton	-	Pro-football player Chicago Bears
Mary L. Smith	-	Interim President Kentucky State University
Gladys J. Willis	-	Chairperson, English Dept. Lincoln University (PA)
Robert G. Clark	-	Politician, Representative, State of Mississippi District 47

MISSISSIPPI VALLEY STATE UNIVERSITY

The University was created by an Act of the Mississippi State Legislature in 1946. It was opened for service to students in the summer of 1950. The first baccalaureate degrees were awarded in 1953 to its first graduating class of 13.

CHRONOLOGY OF NAME CHANGES

1946	-	Mississippi Vocational College
1964	-	Mississippi Valley State College
1974	-	Mississippi Valley State University

THE INSTITUTION

Mississippi Valley is located in the small town of Itta Bena less than 90 miles north of Jackson and about 50 miles from the Arkansas border and the great Mississippi River.

The Address: **Mississippi Valley State University**
Itta Bena, Mississippi 38941
Telephone: (601) 254-9041

The average enrollment is approximately 2000 and the student/faculty ratio is eighteen-to-one.

ACADEMIC PROGRAM

The university has nine departments offering 700 different courses annually and awarding degrees in 30 areas. Students may select majors in the following areas: art/advertisement, biology, business administration, computer science, mathematics, music, education, health, physical education and recreation, industrial technology, social work, speech, environmental health, criminal justice, political/science and government, office administration, sociology, English and visual and performing arts.

Additionally, a cooperative program in oceanography with the Gulf Coast Research Laboratory is available. The university awards the Bachelor of Arts, Bachelor of Science, Bachelor of Music, Master of Science in Environmental Health and Master of Science in Elementary Education.

There are accommodations available for a total of 1914 students in 11 dormitory units. Space is allocated on a first-come first-served basis.

FEES

Cost per academic year: tuition, room and board $4700.

DISTINGUISHED ALUMNI

Fannye E. Love   -   Chairperson, Teacher Education LeMoyne-Owen College

Hampton Smith   -   Professor, Health and Physical Education, Albany State College

RUST COLLEGE

Rust College was founded by the Freedman's Aid Society of the Methodist Episcopal Church at a time when the South had been devastated by the Civil War. Groups such as the Freedman's Aid Society set about providing an education for the newly freed slaves. More than 4000 such schools were established, most failed. Rust survived. It is the oldest historically Black college in the state.

CHRONOLOGY OF NAME CHANGES

1866	-	Shaw School
1870	-	Shaw University
1915	-	Rust College

THE INSTITUTION

The college is located in the north-central part of the state of Mississippi. It is ten miles from the Tennessee border on the north, 50 miles from the Arkansas border on the west and approximately forty-five miles southeast of Memphis, the nearest metropolitan city.

The Address: **Rust College**
Holly Springs, Mississippi 38635
Telephone: (601) 252-4661

Rust College is a coeducational liberal arts institution affiliated with the United Methodist Church. It has an average enrollment of 800 and housing facilities to accommodate approximately 90 percent of the students The student/faculty ratio is twenty-to-one. The campus covers 125 acres and has available thirty-six buildings.

The college awards the Bachelor of Arts degree in 20 majors. Course offerings are organized under five divisions: a sixth division, Freshman Studies, is an interdisciplinary program designed to aid the student in acclimation to college work.

The divisions:
- Business
- Education
- Humanities
- Mass Communication
- Social Sciences
- Science and Mathematics

Dual-degree programs are available: in engineering with Georgia Institute of Technology, Memphis State University, Tuskegee University and University of Mississippi; in health careers with Meharry Medical School; and in nursing with Alcorn State University.

FEES

Cost per academic year: $6000.

DISTINGUISHED ALUMNI

David L. Beckley	-	President, Wiley College
Lonear Heard	-	Owner, McDonald Franchise
Ida L. Jackson	-	First Black teacher, Oakland, CA Public Schools and Eighth Supreme Basileus AKA Sorority
Ida B. Wells	-	An organizer of the NAACP

TOUGALOO COLLEGE

Tougaloo College was founded in 1869 by the American Missionary Society of New York. It is today a private college affiliated with the United Church of Christ and the Christian Church (Disciples of Christ). It offered the first postsecondary level in 1897 and the first baccalaureate degree was awarded in 1901.

CHRONOLOGY OF NAME CHANGES

1869	-	Tougaloo College
1871	-	Tougaloo University
1916	-	Tougaloo College
1954	-	Tougaloo Christian College
1963	-	Tougaloo College

THE INSTITUTION

The college is located in the Jackson metropolitan area. Jackson is the state capital and the largest city in the state. There is available a mass transit bus system and an airport less than 200 miles from campus.

The Address: **Tougaloo College**
Tougaloo, Mississippi 39174
Telephone: (601) 956-4941

The five-hundred-and-nine-acre campus has 14 major buildings and a student enrollment that averages 800. On-campus residence halls house 70 percent of the students.

ACADEMIC PROGRAM

The college offers dual-degree programs, student exchange programs and/or cross-registration with several colleges including Brown University, Georgia Institute of Technology, Howard University, Tuskegee University, University of Mississippi, University of Wisconsin-Madison, Bowdoin College, Meharry Medical College and Millsaps College.

Degrees are offered in accounting, art/advertising, biology, business, chemistry, communications, computer science, economics, education, engineering, English, gerontology, history, humanities, journalism, mathematics, music, physical education, physics, political science, psychology, social welfare, and sociology.

FEES

Cost per academic year: tuition $4500, room and board $2000.

DISTINGUISHED ALUMNI

Dr. Walter Washington	-	President, Alcorn State University
Dr. Oscar A. Rogers, Jr.	-	President, Claflin College
Elaine Baker	-	Professor, Albany State
Terrecia W. Sweet	-	Professor, California State University, Fresno

Missouri

2 H/PBCUs

HARRIS-STOWE STATE COLLEGE

Harris-Stowe State College was founded in 1857 by the St. Louis Public Schools as a Normal school. It was the first public teacher education institution west of the Mississippi River and the twelfth such institution in the United States. Harris-Stowe had two predecessor institutions: The Normal school was originally established for white students only; Stowe Teachers' College, which began in 1890, was the Normal school for black future teachers. The two teacher education institutions were merged by the Board of Education of the St. Louis Public Schools in 1954. This was the first of several steps to integrate the pubic schools of St. Louis.

CHRONOLOGY OF NAME CHANGES

1857	-	Harris Teachers College
1890	-	Stowe Teachers College
1924	-	The Sumner Normal School
1929	-	Stowe Teachers College
1954	-	Harris Teachers College
1979	-	Harris-Stowe State College

THE INSTITUTION

The college is located at the hub of metropolitan St. Louis with access to Interstate Highways 44 and 55 and U.S. Highway 40. It is easily reached by public transportation facilities.

The Address: **Harris-Stowe State College**
3026 - LaClede Avenue
St. Louis, Missouri 63103
Telephone: (314) 533-3000

This is a public coeducational institution, with an average enrollment of 1400 students does not offer dormitories. In 1981, the college received state approval for the Bachelor of Science in Urban Education. This program was at that time the only one of its kind at the undergraduate level in the United States.

ACADEMIC PROGRAM

The programs at Harris-Stowe are devoted exclusively to professional education development, which covers three main fields: teacher development, urban education specialist development and career enrichment. The disciplines addressed at Harris-Stowe are: accounting, aerospace, anthropology/sociology, art, biology, business administration, chemistry, computer science, dance, economics, education, English, French, geography, history, industrial arts, journalism, mathematics, meteorology, philosophy, physical education, physical science, physics, Spanish, speech, theater and urban education.

FEES

Cost per academic year: tuition $5000.

DISTINGUISHED ALUMNI

George Hyram - Vice President, Emeritus Harris-Stowe

LINCOLN UNIVERSITY (MO)

The University was founded by the 62nd and 65th Colored Infantries and their white officers who fought for the Union during the Civil war. It was established as a private school in 1866 and became a state institute in 1879 The first instruction at the postsecondary level was offered in 1877 and the first baccalaureate degree was awarded in 1891.

CHRONOLOGY OF NAME CHANGES

1866 - Lincoln Institute
1921 - Lincoln University

THE INSTITUTION

Lincoln University is located in the capital city of Missouri, Jefferson City. Students attending this university have available all of the benefits of a capital city. Mass transit bus system, an airport twenty-five miles from campus and passenger rail service approximately one mile from campus provide easy access to the campus.

The Address: **Lincoln University**
820 Chestnut Street
Jefferson City, Missouri 65101
Telephone: (314) 681-5000 and 681-5024

In addition to the main campus of 136 acres, the university has a research farm that encompasses more than 800 acres. The public coeducational school has an average enrollment of 4000. On-campus housing can accommodate 50 percent of the students. The student/faculty ratio is twenty-to-one.

The university is a comprehensive, multipurpose campus offering the associate, baccalaureate, and the master's degrees in 55 degree programs: 44 undergraduate and 11 graduate.

The areas of academic concentration are agriculture, business/economics, education, English, fine arts, foreign language, health/physical education, home economics, journalism, natural sciences, nursing science, philosophy, psychology, and social sciences.

FEES

Cost per academic year: tuition $6200.

DISTINGUISHED ALUMNI

Roland Copes   -   Vice President, Human
                                 Resources Division,
                                 Massachusetts Mutual Life
                                 Insurance Company
Dr. Henry Givens, Jr. -   President, Harris-Stowe
                                 State College
Earl Wilson, Jr.   Marketing Director
                                 1994 Olympic Festival
                                 (St. Louis)

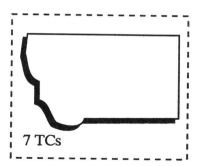

7 TCs

BLACKFEET COMMUNITY COLLEGE

Blackfeet Community College is a coeducational tribally-controlled two-year college. It was chartered in 1974.

THE INSTITUTION

The Address: **Blackfeet Community College**
P.O. Box 819
Browning, Montana 59417
Telephone: (406) 338-5421

The enrollment is approximately 450 students.

DULL KNIFE MEMORIAL COLLEGE

Dull Knife Memorial College was originally chartered in September, 1975, by tribal ordinance as the Northern Cheyenne Indian Action Program. The first academic courses were offered in 1978.

THE INSTITUTION

The College is located on the Northern Cheyenne Reservation in Southeastern Montana, approximately two blocks east and one block north of the intersection of Highways 212 and 39.

The Address: **Dull Knife Memorial College**
P.O. Box 98
Lame Deer, Montana 59043
Telephone: (405) 477-6215

The College has one main building that houses administration, faculty offices, cafeteria facilities, the bookstore and sufficient classroom space to serve 300 students. Two other facilities house the library and the day care center. The adult education center is southwest of the college's main facilities. There are approximately 250 students enrolled at the college.

ACADEMIC PROGRAM

The following degrees are offered:
- Associate of Arts in:
    General Studies
- Associate of Applied Science in:
    Alcohol and Drug Studies, Office Management
    Natural Resources Management
    (this is a degree program which provides specific training in an occupational career field)

FEES

Cost per academic semester: tuition $450.

FORT BELKNAP COMMUNITY COLLEGE

Fort Belknap Community College is a tribally-controlled institution. Founded in 1984, it is primarily a women's college.

THE INSTITUTION

The Address: **Fort Belknap Community College**
P.O. Box 159
Harlem, Montana 59526
Telephone: (406) 853-2607

The College is located in the northeast section of Montana, very near the Canadian border. The school has a student/faculty ratio of eight-to-one. The enrollment is approximately 400 students.

ACADEMIC PROGRAM

FBCC offers the following degrees:
- Associate of Arts
- Associate of Applied Science
- Associate of Applied Science

Majors are available in:
- Business Administration
- Computer Technology
- Construction Technologies
- Data Processing
- Human Services
- Liberal Arts/General Studies
- Secretarial Studies
- Office Management

FEES

Cost per academic semester: tuition $1500.

FORT PECK COMMUNITY COLLEGE

Fort Peck Community College is a tribally-controlled community college chartered by the government of the Fort Peck Assiniboine and Sioux tribes. Courses in higher education were first introduced to the reservation by two state-funded Montana community colleges. In 1986, the Fort Peck Tribes established the Fort Peck Education Department. This department engaged in the development work beginning Fort Peck Community College which was officially chartered in 1978.

THE INSTITUTION

The campus is composed of eight sites which provide about 10,000 square feet of classroom space. It is located near the Canadian border just north of the Missouri River, along US Highway No. 2.

The Address: **Fort Peck Community College**
P.O. Box 575
Poplar, Montana 59255
Telephone: (406) 768-3367

The school has an enrollment of approximately 300 students.

ACADEMIC PROGRAM

The Associate of Arts degree is offered in:
- General Studies
- Liberal arts
- Pre-professional subject areas: Business Administration, Education, Human Services, and Native American studies.

The Associate in Science is awarded in:
- General Studies
- Natural Resources Management

The Associate of Applied Science degree is awarded as a terminal degree in a vocational field. Programs included are:

- Automotive mechanics
- Building trades
- Criminal/civil justice
- Computer operator/graphics
- Electronic technology
- Human Services/Chemical Dependency
- Office Technology
- Tribal Administration

FEES

Cost per academic year: $900.

LITTLE BIG HORN COLLEGE

Little Big Horn College is an independent two-year coeducational college that was chartered in 1980.

THE INSTITUTION

The Address: **Little Big Horn College**
P.O. Box 370
Crow Agency, Montana 59022
Telephone: (406) 638-2228

The 5-acre rural campus has an enrollment of 220 students.

ACADEMIC PROGRAM

The Associates of Applied Science is offered in the following areas:
- Business Administration
- Carpentry
- Computer Science
- Elementary Education
- Liberal Arts/General Studies
- Mathematics
- Science

FEES

Fee information was unavailable at time of printing. Please contact the college at the above address for current tuition costs.

SALISH KOOTENAI COLLEGE

Salish Kootenai College is a four-year tribal college founded in 1977. It serves primarily members of the Salish and Kootenai Tribes located in five reservation towns: Polson, Ronan, St. Ignatius, Arlee and Hot Springs. Formal education for the members of the Salish and Kootenai Tribes began with federal government contracts with parochial schools, public schools and off-reservation boarding schools. The results were not acceptable, few Indian people graduated from High school and even fewer graduated from college. In an attempt to improve education, the Tribal Council established Two Eagle River School, which serves grades 9 to 12 and Salish Kootenai College.

THE INSTITUTION

The Address: **Salish Kootenai College**
P.O. Box 117, Highway 93
Pablo, Montana 59855
Telephone: (406) 675-4800

The College is located in the center of the Flathead Indian Reservation in western Montana. The campus is located east of Highway 93, opposite the Tribal Office Complex in Pablo, Montana. The Flathead Reservation is surrounded on the east, west and south by mountains. To the north is Flathead Lake, the largest natural freshwater late of the Mississippi River. The beautiful Flathead River winds its way through the reservation from north to south bisecting it. Within the reservation's boundaries are the National Bison Range and the Ninepipe National Wildlife Refuge. Also, nearby western Montana area are Glacier National Park, the Bob Marshall Wilderness Area, the Lolo National Forest and the Flathead National Forest.

The College has an enrollment of 740 students.

ACADEMIC PROGRAM

Salish Kootenai College offers the following:
- Bachelor of Arts Degree
    Human Services Rehabilitation
- Associate of Arts
    Chemical Dependency
    General Studies/Liberal Arts Option
    Human Services
    Native American Studies
- Associate of Science
    Environmental Science
    Forestry Technology
    General Studies/Science Option
    Health Records Technology
    Information Systems
    Nursing
- Associate of Applied Science
    Dental Assisting Technology
    Office Education
- Certificate of Completion
    Bilingual Education
    Building Trades
    Dental Assisting Technology
    Native American Studies
    Office Education

FEES

Cost per academic quarter: tuition $1800.

STONE CHILD COLLEGE

Stone Child College, a tribally-controlled community college, was chartered by the Chippewa-Cree Business Committee on May 17, 1984. The reservation was founded by Chiefs Rocky Boy and Little Bear. Rocky Boy was the last Indian reservation established in Montana.

Rocky Boy's people were among a number of Chippewa Indians who originated in the Great Lakes region. Chief Little Bear was considered a Canadian Cree. The reservation lies in the shadows and scenic area of the Bear Paw Mountains of north central Montana and includes country of rolling foothills and prairie land.

THE INSTITUTION

The Address: **Stone Child College**
P.O. Box 1082 Rocky Bay Route
Box Elder, Montana 59521
Telephone: (406) 395-4313

The College is fourteen miles from Box Elder, Montana. The campus is relatively isolated which probably accounts for the rich cultural heritage continuing on the Rocky Boy Reservation. The college has an enrollment of approximately 150 students.

ACADEMIC PROGRAM

Students select courses from three areas:
- Requirement for the Major
- General Education/Related Instruction Requirements
- Electives

Degrees and certificates are awarded in the following areas:

- Associates of Arts
  - General Studies
    - Liberal Arts Option
      - Mathematics/Science Option
      - Earth Systems Concentration
      - Math/Engineering Concentration
    - Native American Studies Option
    - Teach Education Option
  - Human Services
    - Technology Option
    - Chemical Dependency Option
- Associate of Science
  - General Business
    - General Business Option
    - Tribal Management Option
  - Secretarial Science
    - Clerical
  - Computer Science
    - Computer Office Skills Concentration
    - Information Systems Concentration
    - Publications/Graphics Concentration
- Certificates of Completion
  - Building Trades
  - Secretarial Science

FEES

Cost per academic year: tuition and fees $8950.

 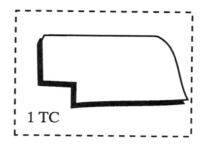

NEBRASKA INDIAN COMMUNITY COLLEGE

Nebraska Indian Community College is an independent two-year coeducational college.

THE INSTITUTION

The Address: **Nebraska Indian Community College**
Winnebago, Nebraska 68071
Telephone: (402) 878-2414

The College has an enrollment of 222 students.

ACADEMIC PROGRAM

The degrees awarded are Associate of Arts, The Associate of Science and the Associate of Applied Science.

Majors are available in the following areas:
- Business Administration
- Computer Science
- Criminal Justice

- Drug and Alcohol Abuse Counseling
- Education
- Electrical and Electronics Technologies
- Gerontology
- Human Services
- Liberal Arts/General Studies
- Native American Studies
- Natural Resource Management
- Plumbing
- Public Administration
- Secretarial Studies/Office Management

FEES

Cost per academic year: tuition and fees $1800.

1 H/PBCU

BLOOMFIELD COLLEGE

Bloomfield College was established in the mid 1800s as a training school for German speaking ministers. Today, it is a liberal arts college affiliated with the Presbyterian church.

CHRONOLOGY OF NAME CHANGES

1868 - German Theological Seminary of Newark
1913 - Bloomfield Theological Seminary
1926 - Bloomfield College and Seminary
1961 - Bloomfield College

THE INSTITUTION

Bloomfield college is located in the northern section of the state of New Jersey. It is approximately ten miles northwest of Newark and 5 miles west of New York City. Transportation to and from the campus is provided by bus, train and air. Bus service from the campus to the airport and/or the train station is readily available. Its proximity to New York makes this a very exciting campus.

The Address: **Bloomfield College**
Bloomfield, New Jersey 07003
Telephone: (201) 748-9000

On-campus living is available in residence halls, fraternity and sorority houses, and the Honors house. The school also operates several off-campus apartments to accommodate students. Priority for on-campus housing is given to freshmen. The enrollment is approximately 2000.

ACADEMIC PROGRAM

The campus offers the Bachelor of Arts degree in economics, English, fine and performing arts, French, history, interdisciplinary studies, philosophy, religion, sociology and Spanish.

The Bachelor of Science degree is available in accounting, biology, business administration, chemistry and nursing.

FEES

Cost per academic year: tuition $7400, room and board $3800.

DISTINGUISHED ALUMNI

Juan Simpson	-	New Products Controller, Johnson & Johnson, Piscataway, N.J.
Manuel Suarez	-	Professor of Modern Language University of the Virgin Islands
Frances Antonia	-	Judge, Superior Court New Jersey

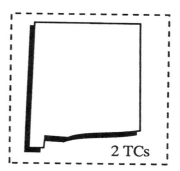

2 TCs

CROWNPOINT INSTITUTE OF TECHNOLOGY

Crownpoint Institute of Technology, chartered by the Navajo Nation, was founded in 1979. It is a two-year coeducational institute. The objective of the institute is to equip students with technical/vocational skills, by providing high quality and relevant programs and services. Though the institute is primarily oriented toward the people of the Navajo Nation, all are welcome.

THE INSTITUTION

The Address: **Crownpoint Institute of Technology**
Crownpoint, New Mexico 87313
Telephone: (505) 786-5851
(1-800) 343-4891

On-campus housing is available for approximately 100 students is awarded on a first-come first-served basis. Enrollment is approximately 200 students.

ACADEMIC PROGRAM

Certificate of Completion is awarded in the following programs:
- Accounting
- Applied Computer Technology
- Building Maintenance
- Carpentry
- Culinary Arts
- Electrical Trades
- Heavy Equipment Mechanics
- Livestock and Range Management
- Nursing Assistance
- Plumbing and Pipe Fitting
- Secretarial Science
- Surveying Technology

FEES

Cost per academic year: tuition, fees, room and board $3600.

INSTITUTE OF AMERICAN INDIAN ARTS

The Institute of American Indian Arts is a federally supported two-year coeducational college, founded in 1962.

THE INSTITUTION

The Address:　　**Institute of American Indian Arts**
College of Santa Fe Campus
P.O. Box 20007
St. Michael's Drive
Santa Fe, New Mexico 87801-9990
Telephone: (505) 988-6495

The Institute is an 100-acre urban campus with an enrollment of 250 students. Housing is available for 140 students on a first-come first-served basis.

ACADEMIC PROGRAM

The Associate Degree is awarded in the following areas:
- Art/Fine Arts
- Ceramic Art and Design
- Creative Writing
- Dance
- Fashion Design and Technology
- Jewelry and Metalsmithing
- Museum Studies
- Music
- Painting/Drawing
- Photography
- Sculpture

- Studio Art
- Textile Arts
- Theater Arts/Drama

FEES

Cost per academic year: tuition $2000, room and board $3200.

2 H/PBCU's

AUDREY COHEN COLLEGE

In 1964, Audrey C. Cohen founded the College for Human Services and the college was charted in 1970. It was described as a new kind of educational institution. At the College for Human Services emphasis was turned from an economy based on manufacturing toward an economy based on service. The mission of the college is to provide the kind of education needed for service-oriented corporations and businesses. In 1984 the college received full accreditation as a pioneer in education for the new economy.

CHRONOLOGY OF NAME CHANGES

    1964 - College for Human Services
    1993 - Audrey Cohen College

THE INSTITUTION

The College's main location is in New York City, specifically in Manhattan, near Greenwich Village, the financial district, and SoHo's artistic community. It is convenient to all public transportation.

The Address: **Audrey Cohen College**
345 Hudson Street
New York, New York 10014
Telephone: (212) 989-2002

The keystone of the College is academic programs that respond to the question, What must professionals be able to do in this new economy, and how can they prepare for demanding and changing roles? The College started with less than 300 students. The current enrollment averages 2000. Audrey Cohen College offers three semesters annually and is primarily a commuter college.

ACADEMIC PROGRAM

The college offers a performance-based baccalaureate program which can be completed in two years and eight months. The Bachelor of Professional Studies is awarded in business and human services. The College also offers a three-semester Master of Science degree program which can be completed in one calendar year.

Through the Advanced Standing Option, students with significant work experience plus related educational courses may be able to apply their demonstrated past experience to the College system requirements. These students may be granted exemption from up to three semesters. Also, transfer applicants to undergraduate programs may be able to receive transfer credit for related individual courses.

FEES

Cost per academic semester:
tuition $3600 School of Human Services
$3800 School of Business
$ 930 Additional for participation in the
Advanced Standing Program

MEDGAR EVERS COLLEGE (CUNY)

Medgar Evers College, founded in 1969 as a result of community efforts, is named in memory of the slain civil rights leader. The College was established to meet the educational needs of the Central Brooklyn community from which it draws 85 percent of its students. The student population is 92 percent black, and includes people with roots in seventy-five countries including the Caribbean and Africa. Approximately 71 percent of the student population is female and more than 50 percent of the student population is 25 years or older. The College's mission is to provide high quality, professional, career-oriented undergraduate degree programs within the context of a liberal arts curriculum, through the offering of both associates and baccalaureate degrees.

THE INSTITUTION

Situated in Central Brooklyn, access to Medgar Evers College is readily available. The multifaceted nature of New York City's mass transit system (bus, subway and taxis) minimize the necessity to have a car. The multi-cultural diversification of the neighborhood in which Medgar Evers is located, compliments the diversity in the classroom as well as the environment surrounding the institution.

The Address: **Medgar Evers College (CUNY)**
1650 Bedford Avenue
Brooklyn, New York 11225
Telephone: (718) 270-4900 or 270-6000

The coeducational institution is one of 17 colleges within the City University of New York System. Enrollment averages 4600 students, however, there are no on-campus housing facilities.

ACADEMIC PROGRAM

A broad range of course offerings is available as major areas of concentration. The college offers 8 baccalaureate degree programs in accounting, business administration, nursing, public administration, biology, elementary education, special education, and psychology. Soon to be added to the baccalaureate degree offerings will be the bachelor's degree in mathematics and environmental science. Associate degree programs are offered in the following areas: secretarial science, computer applications, business administration, liberal arts (humanities and social sciences), nursing science, public administration, and elementary education.

The College has a number of special Centers and programs designed to assist students in the successful completion of their academic endeavors including: The Center for Law and Social Justice, The Caribbean Research Center, The Center for Women's Development, The Center for the Study and Resolution of Black and Latino Male Initiatives, the Jackie Robinson Center for Physical Culture and the Ralph Bunche Center for Public Policy.

FEES

Cost per academic semester: tuition $1400.

DISTINGUISHED ALUMNI/STAFF

Dr. Betty Shabazz - Wife of Malcolm Shabazz (Malcolm X)
                    A member of the College staff.
Alford A. Smith, M.D. - Medical Director
                    Flatbush Family Practice

 *North Carolina*

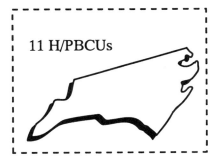 11 H/PBCUs

BARBER-SCOTIA COLLEGE

Founded in 1867 by Reverend Luke Dorland, Barber-Scotia College is a four-year independent coeducational institution affiliated with the Presbyterian Church. The original mission of the college was to train young Negro women as teachers and as social workers. In 1930, Barber Memorial merged with Scotia Women's College and in 1954, the College became coeducational.

CHRONOLOGY OF NAME CHANGES

1867	-	Scotia Seminary
1916	-	Scotia Women's College
1932	-	Barber-Scotia College

THE INSTITUTION

Barber-Scotia is located in Concord, North Carolina, a city of approximately 30,000. It is served by Southern Railway; Charlotte-Douglas International Airport is only 30 miles away.

The Address: **Barber-Scotia College**
145 Cabarrus Avenue
Concord, North Carolina 28025
Telephone: (704) 786-5171

Twenty-five buildings are nestled on the forty-acre campus together with tennis courts, athletic and recreational areas. The small
college, with nearly 800 students, provides comfortable and modern on-campus housing for ninety-five percent of the student body
The students come from 15 or more states, as well as the District of
Columbia, the U.S. Virgin Islands, Africa and other countries. Over
50 percent of the faculty at Barber-Scotia have received doctoral
degrees and the students enjoy a student/faculty ratio of ten-to-one.

ACADEMIC PROGRAM

The college offers the Bachelor of Science and the Bachelor of Arts
degrees. Majors are available in: accounting, banking, biology,
business administration, communication and journalism, computer
science, education, English, health and physical education, hospitality management, mathematics, marketing finance, medical technology, pre-engineering, recreation administration, sociology and
straight chiropractic.

FEES

Cost per academic year: tuition, room and board $7000.

DISTINGUISHED ALUMNI

Mary McLeod Bethune	-	Founder, President National Council of Negro Women
Eula Saxon Dean, Ph.D.	-	Dean, Cosumnes River College
Mable Parker McLean	-	Former President Barber-Scotia College
Mable Phiefer, Ph.D.	-	Owner, Black College Network

BENNETT COLLEGE

Established in 1873 as a coeducational institution, the Freedman's Aid and Southern Education Society of the Methodist Episcopal Church assumed the initial responsibility for the support of the school. Chartered as a college in 1889 and reorganized as a college for women in 1926, Bennett is a private college affiliated with the United Methodist Church. It was one of the first Black colleges to be admitted into full membership in the Southern Association of Colleges and Secondary Schools.

CHRONOLOGY OF NAME CHANGES

    1873 - Bennett Seminary
    1889 - Bennett College

THE INSTITUTION

The campus is located approximately 65 miles west of Raleigh, the state capital. It is 30 miles from the Virginia border, situated in the north-central section of North Carolina. The municipal bus system and a passenger rail service is available to the campus.

The Address: **Bennett College**
900 East Washington Street
Greensboro, North Carolina 27401-3239
Telephone: (919) 370-8624
Toll-free: 1-800-338-Benn

The average enrollment is 600 women and forty-six percent of the students are from North Carolina and others are from throughout the United Stated and six foreign countries. Located on the fifty-five-acre campus are twenty-four buildings, including seven residence halls with professional and peer staff. The average class has 20 students and there is a student/faculty ratio of eleven-to-one. As an institution for women, Bennett affords women the environment in which they are freer to develop personally, intellectually, and professionally - as individuals, scholars and leaders.

ACADEMIC PROGRAM

The Liberal Arts college has four major divisions: Education, Humanities, Social Science, and Natural Sciences. The bachelor's degree is offered in accounting, biology, business administration, chemistry, computer science, English, home economics, mathematics, political science, psychology and the health professions including nursing. Dual-degree and/or cooperative education programs are available with the following institutions:

- North Carolina Agricultural and Technical State University
- University of North Carolina - Chapel Hill
- Bowman Gray School of Medicine
- Howard University Hospital

FEES

Cost per academic year: tuition, room and board $7500.

DISTINGUISHED ALUMNI

Carolyn Robertson Payton - 1st Female Director of the U.S. Peace Corp.

Dorothy Lavinia Brown - 1st African-American Female Surgeon in the South

Rev. Jacquelyn Grant - Professor, Interdenominational Theological Center

Celestine Wilson Goodloe - Assoc. Director of Admission Xavier (OH)

ELIZABETH CITY STATE UNIVERSITY

Established as Elizabeth City State Colored Normal School in 1891, the university offered the first instruction at the postsecondary level in 1937. The first baccalaureate degree was awarded in 1939.

CHRONOLOGY OF NAME CHANGES

1891	-	Elizabeth City State Colored Normal School
1939	-	Elizabeth City State Teachers College
1963	-	Elizabeth City State College
1969	-	Elizabeth City State University

THE INSTITUTION

The campus of 160 acres is located in the far northeast corner of the state of North Carolina and less than 50 miles from Norfolk, Virginia. There is access to water ways that lead to the Albemarle Sound. The city is served by an airport 50 miles away as well as rail and bus service.

The Address: **Elizabeth City State University**
1704 Weeksville Road
Elizabeth City, North Carolina 27909
Telephone: (919) 335-3400 and 335-3305

Elizabeth City State is a public coeducational institution. The available housing will accommodate 50 percent of the average enrollment of 2000 students. The campus enjoys a twelve-to-one student/faculty ratio.

ACADEMIC PROGRAM

The academic units of the University consist of two divisions:
Division of General Studies
Division of Education

There are twelve departments: art, biology, business and economics, geosciences, language, literature and communication, mathematics and computer science, military science, music, physical education and health, physical science, social science and technology.

The baccalaureate degree is awarded in a number of majors including art, biological sciences, broadcasting, business and management, chemistry, computer and information sciences, criminal justice, education, English, fine and applied arts, mathematics, music, physical sciences, psychology, public affairs and social sciences.

The option is also available to participate in joint programs with the Norfolk State University and North Carolina State University.

FEES

Cost per academic year: tuition, room and board $9200.

DISTINGUISHED ALUMNI

Dr. Jimmy R. Jenkins - 1st Alumnus to become Chancellor of Elizabeth City State University

Dr. Curtis E. Bryan - President, Denmark Technical College (S.C.)

Dr. Leonard Slade, Jr. - Dean, College of Arts & Science Kentucky State College

FAYETTEVILLE STATE UNIVERSITY

The University, originally established as Howard School in 1867 was designed to serve Colored people. It offered the first instruction at the postsecondary level in 1921 and is now a part of the University of North Carolina system.

CHRONOLOGY OF NAME CHANGES

1867	-	Howard School
1916	-	State Colored Normal and Industrial School
1921	-	State Normal School for the Negro Race
1926	-	State Normal School
1939	-	Fayetteville State Teachers College
1963	-	Fayetteville State College
1969	-	Fayetteville State University

THE INSTITUTION

Fayetteville State is located 50 miles from Raleigh and Durham, the nearest metropolitan areas. The university is served by mass transit bus system, an airport eight miles from campus and passenger rail service four miles from campus.

The Address: **Fayetteville State University**
Murchinson Road
Fayetteville, North Carolina 28301
Telephone: (919) 486-1371
1-800-222-2594

The campus spreads over 156 acres between Raleigh and Durham, with a student body population of 4000 and a student/faculty ratio of nineteen-to-one. On-campus residence halls house forty-eight percent of the students.

ACADEMIC PROGRAM

The public coeducational institution offers the associate, the bacca-laureate and the master's degrees. Major areas of study include biological sciences, business and management, education, fine and applied arts, mathematics physical sciences, psychology, public affairs and service, and social sciences.

Fort Bragg-Pope Air Force Base, less than 30 miles from the main campus, is the site for Servicemembers Opportunity College. The university offers the cooperative baccalaureate program in engineering with North Carolina State University at Raleigh and in medical technology with approved hospitals. Institutionally-sponsored study abroad is available.

FEES

Cost per academic year: tuition $5800, room and board $2500.

DISTINGUISHED ALUMNI

Algeania Freeman	-	Dept. Chair, Community Health & Rehabilitation, Norfolk State
Gerald Sullivan	-	Professor, Military Science Dillard University
Jerry C. Johnson	-	Athletic Director, LeMoyne-Owen College

JOHNSON C. SMITH UNIVERSITY

Johnson C. Smith was established in 1867 as a private men's institution affiliated with the Presbyterian Church. The school was charted in 1869, awarded its first baccalaureate degree in 1872 and became fully coeducational in 1941.

CHRONOLOGY OF NAME CHANGES

1867 - Biddle Memorial Institute
1876 - Biddle University
1923 - Johnson C. Smith University

THE INSTITUTION

The university is located in Charlotte and enjoys the transportation options that are available in a city of nearly one million people.

The Address: **Johnson C. Smith**
                 100-300 Bettieford Road
                 Charlotte, North Carolina 28216
                 Telephone: (704) 378-1041 and 378-1010

The campus has 21 buildings located on 100 acres and approximately 1200 students in attendance. On-campus housing is available.

ACADEMIC PROGRAM

Joint degree program in engineering with University of North Carolina and in marine biology with Duke are options available for the students. The curriculum offers majors in English, foreign language, fine arts and humanities, business administration and economics, history and political science, sociology and social work, education, health and physical education, psychology, biology, chemistry, physics, computer science and mathematics. The student/faculty ratio is fifteen-to-one.

FEES

Cost per academic year: tuition $6000, room and board $2500.

DISTINGUISHED ALUMNI

Richard C. Erwin	- U.S. District Judge, Middle District, North Carolina. 1st African-American to win statewide race for an elected office.
Lucy Allen	- Director, Center for Educational Technology University of the Virgin Islands
Mildred Mitchell-Bateman	- West Virginia's 1st Black Department Head - (Dept. of Mental Health)

LIVINGSTONE COLLEGE

The college was founded by African Methodist Episcopal Zion Church in 1879 and named for David Livingstone, the missionary, explorer and philanthropist. The first postsecondary level instruction was offered in 1880 and the first baccalaureate degree was awarded in 1887.

CHRONOLOGY OF NAME CHANGES

1879	-	Zion Wesley Institute
1885	-	Zion Wesley College
1887	-	Livingstone College

THE INSTITUTION

The campus encompasses 18 buildings and is located 60 miles from Charlotte, the nearest metropolitan area. The campus is served by an airport 50 miles away.

The Address: **Livingstone College**
701 West Monroe Street
Salisbury, North Carolina 28144
Telephone: (704) 638-5502

The enrollment averages 600 and the student/faculty ratio is ten-to-one. On-campus residence halls house seventy-six percent of the student body.

ACADEMIC PROGRAM

The college consists of two schools: an undergraduate college of arts and science and a graduate school of theology (Hood Theological Seminary). The undergraduate liberal arts college has four divisions:

- Business
- Humanities
- Natural Sciences
- Social and Behavioral Sciences

Three degrees are conferred: Bachelor of Arts, Bachelor of Science and Bachelor of Social Work.

Dual-degree programs are offered in engineering with Georgia Institute of Technology and Clemson University. Professional training for the ministry leading to the Master of Divinity and the Master of Religious Education is available through Hood Theological Seminary.

FEES

Cost per academic year: tuition, room and board $8600.

DISTINGUISHED ALUMNI

Elizabeth Koontz	-	Formerly President National Education Association and Director, Women's Bureau Dept. and Labor
Alfred Leroy Edwards	-	Deputy Assistant Secretary of Agriculture, 1963
Dr. Roy Hudson	-	Corporate Vice-President Public Relations The Upjohn Co.
Dr. James Gavin, III	-	Senior Scientific Officer Howard Hughes Medical Inst. President-Elect American Diabetes Assoc.

NORTH CAROLINA AGRICULTURAL AND TECHNICAL STATE UNIVERSITY

The first instruction at the college was in Raleigh in 1891 as an annex of Shaw University. The first baccalaureate degree was awarded in 1893. The institute was moved from Raleigh to Greensboro in 1896 and became a part of the state system in 1972.

CHRONOLOGY OF NAME CHANGES

1891 - A and M College for the Colored Race
1915 - Agricultural and Technical College of North Carolina
1967 - North Carolina Agricultural and Technical State University

THE INSTITUTION

Located between Raleigh and Winston-Salem, the college is served by mass transit bus system, an airport 12 miles away and passenger rail service less than five miles from campus.

The Address: **North Carolina A & T State University**
1601 Market Street
Greensboro, North Carolina 27411
Telephone: (919) 334-7500

The enrollment at the campus averages 7600 students and campus housing can accommodate fifty-one percent of the students. The student/faculty ratio is fifteen-to-one.

ACADEMIC PROGRAM

The university consists of seven schools:
- Agriculture
- Arts and Science

- Business and Economics
- Education
- Engineering
- Nursing
- Graduate Studies

The majors available through the seven schools include accounting, agribusiness, animal science, business administration, child/family development, computer science, drama, economics, education, engineering, home economics, landscaping, music, nursing, physics, political science, psychology, sociology, social work and speech.

FEES

Cost per academic year: tuition $5700, room and board $2500.

DISTINGUISHED ALUMNI

Ronald McNair	-	NASA Astronaut and Mission Specialist
Rev. Jesse L. Jackson	-	Minister, Civil Rights Activist President, National Rainbow Coalition
Frances Huntly-Cooper	-	Mayor, Fitchburg, WI
Robert C. Weaver	-	First African-American U.S. Government cabinet member
Ann Watts McKinney	-	Dean, Graduate Studies Norfolk State University
Thomas Alex Farringon	-	President, Input Output Computer Services (MA)
Dr. Willie C. Robinson	-	President Florida Memorial College

NORTH CAROLINA CENTRAL UNIVERSITY

Originally chartered as a private religious training school, the university was changed to a state institution in 1923. The first instruction at the postsecondary level was in 1910 and the first baccalaureate was awarded in 1929. The university became a part of University of North Carolina System in 1972.

CHRONOLOGY OF NAME CHANGES

1909 - National Religious Training School and Chatauga
1915 - National Training School
1923 - Durham State Normal School
1925 - North Carolina College for Negroes
1947 - North Carolina College at Durham
1969 - North Carolina Central University

THE INSTITUTION

The university is located in the Raleigh-Durham metropolitan area and is served by a mass transit system as well as an airport and passenger rail service within 20 miles of the campus.

The Address: **North Carolina Central University**
1801 Fayetteville Street
Durham, North Carolina 27707
Telephone: (919) 560-6100

On-campus living is available for thirty-eight percent of the average enrollment of 5600 students. Housing is also available for married students on a first-come first-served basis. The campus area with 60 buildings covers 72 of the total 101 acres.

ACADEMIC PROGRAM

The degrees awarded are bachelor's, first professional (law) and master's. The student/faculty ratio is twenty-to-one.

Degrees are awarded in the following areas: accounting, art/advertising, business administration, chemistry, computer sciences, counseling/student personnel, criminal justice, drama, economics, education, English, fine arts, food science and technology, foreign language, geography, health and physical education, history, home economics, library science, mathematics, music, nursing, philosophy, physics, political science and government, pre-medicine, psychology, public administration, social studies, and speech correction.

Also available is the option to participate in dual-degree programs with Georgia Institute of Technology.

FEES

Cost per academic year: tuition $5000, room and board $3000.

DISTINGUISHED ALUMNI

Daniel T. Blue, Jr.	-	Speaker of the House, State of North Carolina
Carolyn G. Morris	-	Deputy Asst. Director the FBI's highest ranking woman 1986
Dr. S. Dallas Simmons	-	9th President, Virginia Union University
Dr. Cleon Thompson, Jr.	-	Chancellor, Winston-Salem State University
Dr. B. Marshall Henderson	-	Chairperson, Biology Dept. Lincoln University (PA)
Robert Massey	-	Professional Football Player

SAINT AUGUSTINE'S COLLEGE

Saint Augustine's was established in 1867 as a private college affiliated with the Episcopal Church. The first postsecondary level instructions were offered in 1919. The school became a four-year institute in 1927 and the first baccalaureate was awarded in 1931.

CHRONOLOGY OF NAME CHANGES

1867 - Saint Augustine's Normal School and Collegiate Institute
1893 - Saint Augustine's School
1919 - Saint Augustine's Junior College
1928 - Saint Augustine's College

THE INSTITUTION

The college is located in the Raleigh-Durham area, which is in the central part of North Carolina. The airport is 15 miles from the campus and passenger rail service is less than a mile from campus.

The Address: **Saint Augustine's College**
1315 Oakwood Avenue
Raleigh, North Carolina 27611
Telephone: (919) 828-4451

The college has an average enrollment of 1800 students and offers housing to accommodate seventy-five percent of the student body. Thirty-six buildings provide modern facilities for learning and living. The student/faculty ratio is fifteen-to-one.

ACADEMIC PROGRAM

The campus is spread over 110 acres. The structure of the academic program consists of five divisions:

- Business
- Humanities
- Education
- Natural Sciences
- Social Sciences

Each division has its own faculty and offers a choice of majors leading to either the Bachelor of Arts or the Bachelor of Science degree.

For the Bachelor of Arts degree, the majors provided include art, communication media, education, English, history and government, language arts, music, political science, psychology, social studies, sociology and social welfare, and urban studies.

For the Bachelor of Science degree, the majors provided are accounting, biology, business, chemistry, computer science, criminal justice, economics, health and physical education, industrial hygiene and safety, mathematics, medical technology, physics, physical therapy, civil engineering, electrical engineering, materials engineering, aerospace engineering, mechanical engineering, industrial engineering, biological and agricultural engineering, chemical engineering, and pre-medicine.

FEES

Cost per academic year: tuition, room and board $8700.

DISTINGUISHED ALUMNI

William S. Thompson	-	Senior Judge, Superior Court District of Columbia
Dr. LeVerne McCummings	-	Former President, Cheney University, (PA)
Dr. Prezell R. Robinson	-	President, St. Augustine's College

SHAW UNIVERSITY

Shaw University is a private institution affiliated with the Baptist Church and founded in 1865. The first instruction at the postsecondary level was offered in 1874. The first baccalaureate degree was awarded in 1878.

CHRONOLOGY OF NAME CHANGES

1865 - Raleigh Institute
1870 - Shaw Collegiate Institute
1875 - Shaw University

THE INSTITUTION

The university is located in Raleigh, the capital city of North Carolina. The campus is less than 60 miles from the Virginia state border. Location in the capital city ensures the campus of a mass transit bus system, an airport with easy accessibility and passenger rail service less than two miles from campus.

The Address: **Shaw University**
                 118 East South Street
                 Raleigh, North Carolina 27611
                 Telephone: (919) 546-8200

Shaw has an average enrollment of 2000 students and provides on-campus housing for 60 percent of the student body. The student/faculty ratio is twenty-five-to-one and students are provided the opportunity to study abroad in the Middle Eastern countries.

ACADEMIC PROGRAM

Degrees are offered in the following areas: accounting, business administration, communication, computer science, criminal justice, drama, education, health and physical education, mathematics, music, physical therapy, public administration, psychology and sociology.

FEES

Cost per academic year: tuition $4500, room and board $3200.

DISTINGUISHED ALUMNI

James E. Cheek	-	Youngest President of Shaw and Howard Universities
David C. Linton	-	Vice President Black Music Division Warner Communications
Marianne T. Johnson	-	Asst. Director of Admissions Lincoln University (PA)
Dr. Collie Coleman	-	President, Allen University

WINSTON-SALEM STATE UNIVERSITY

Established as an industrial academy in 1892, the first postsecondary level instruction was offered in 1925. The institution awarded the first baccalaureate degree in 1927. It is a public coeducational institution, a constituent of the University of North Carolina.

CHRONOLOGY OF NAME CHANGES

1892	-	Slater Industrial Academy
1899	-	Slater Industrial & State Normal School
1925	-	Winston-Salem Teacher College
1963	-	Winston-Salem State College
1969	-	Winston-Salem State University

THE INSTITUTION

The 94-acre campus is located in Winston-Salem, about 70 miles north of Charlotte. Winston-Salem is a relatively large metropolitan area served by a mass transit bus system and two airports.

The Address: **Winston-Salem State University**
601 Martin Luther King, Jr. Dr.
Winston-Salem, North Carolina 27110
Telephone: (919) 750-2000

The university has an average enrollment of 2600 students, fifty-five percent of these students can be housed on campus. The student/faculty ratio is fifteen-to-one.

ACADEMIC PROGRAM

Each freshman and sophomore enrollee is initially admitted as a general studies student. Upon completing forty-seven required course credits, the student may be formally admitted to a specific academic program. The undergraduate degree options are available in more than thirty majors. This would include majors in accounting, applied science, art, biology, business administration, business education, chemistry, computer science, economics, early childhood education, secondary education, English, history, mass communication, mathematics, medical technology, music education, nursing, office administration, physical education, political science, psychology, recreation therapy, secretarial and related programs, sociology, Spanish, special education, sports management, and urban affairs.

Through the Center for Graduate Studies, the Masters is available in business administration, educational administration, elementary education and middle grade education.

FEES

Cost per academic year: tuition $4000, room and board $2500.

DISTINGUISHED ALUMNI

Dr. Calvert H. Smith	-	President, Morris Brown College
Dr. Thomas Monteiro	-	Chairman, School of Education, Brooklyn College
Joyce Owens Pettis	-	Asst. Professor of English North Carolina State Univ.
Dr. Thomas Gunnings	-	Professor of Psychiatry Michigan State University

FORT BERTHOLD COMMUNITY COLLEGE

Fort Berthold Community College was founded May 2, 1973. It is tribally chartered by the three affiliated tribes of the Fort Berthold Reservation headquartered in New Town, North Dakota. The mission of the college is to address tribal needs and concerns, and to perpetuate tribal heritage, history and culture through education.

THE INSTITUTION

The Address: **Fort Berthold Community College**
P.O. Box 490
New Town, North Dakota 58763
Telephone: (701) 627-4738 or 627-3665

The College is located near the scenic Lake Sakakawea area.

ACADEMIC PROGRAM

The college offers programs of study leading to the Associate of

Arts degree, Associate of Science and Associate in Applied Science degrees, as well as Vocational Certificates of Completion.

The Associate of Arts program is designed to provide instruction that leads to credits transferable to other institutions of higher education. Each degree program requires a minimum of sixty-four credit hours. Programs are available in liberal arts with an emphasis on special education, accounting, business administration, public/ tribal administration and human services.

The Associate of Science is offered in nursing.

The Associate in Applied Science is designed to lead the individual directly to employment in a specific career. Program are offered in carpentry, marketing/management, farm/ranch management, information management specialist, and medical secretary.

Vocational certificates are available in clerical, secretarial, marketing/management, carpentry, farm/ranch management, home health care technician and nursing assistant program.

FEES

Cost per academic year: tuition, room and board $5000.

LITTLE HOOP COMMUNITY COLLEGE

Little Hoop Community College is a tribally chartered college serving residents and communities on and near the Devils Lake Sioux Reservation, Fort Totten, North Dakota. The college was founded in October, 1974. In the spring of 1975, the first classes were offered. From 1974 to 1981, the college operated as a satellite of Lake Region Community College. In 1981, Little Hoop Community College became an autonomous higher education institution.

THE INSTITUTION

The Address:　**Little Hoop Community College**
P.O. Box 269
Fort Totten, North Dakota 58335
Telephone: (701) 766-4415

ACADEMIC PROGRAM

Little Hoop Community College offers course work leading to associate degrees in the following areas:

- Associate of Arts: Liberal Arts

- Associate of Science:
  - Accounting
  - Child Development
  - Fish and Wildlife Management
  - Industrial Management
  - Mid-management
  - Office Education
  - Small Business/Entrepreneurship
  - Tribal Administration
  - Bilingual Education
  - Computer Programming
  - Industrial Technology
  - Office Systems

- Vocational Education Certification in:

Adult Basic Education	Basic Carpentry
Basic Wiring	Building Care
Computer Programming	Fish and Wildlife
General Secretarial	Industrial Management
Industrial Technology	Marketing
Mechanical Systems	Mid-management
Pre-Employment Skills	Receptionist
Small Business/Entrepreneurship	
Small Engine Repair	

FEES

Tuition is $45. per unit. For a full time student with 12 units, the total cost would be $1080/year. For students carrying 6 units, the total cost is $540. Books and laboratory fees could add an additional $300 to $400 per year.

STANDING ROCK COLLEGE

Standing Rock College is an independent two-year coeducational college founded in 1973.

THE INSTITUTION

The Address: **Standing Rock College**
Fort Yates, North Dakota 58538
Telephone: (701) 854-3864

The College has an enrollment of approximately 220 students.

ACADEMIC PROGRAM

The degrees offered include the Associate of Arts, Associate of Science and the Associate in Applied Science.

Degrees are awarded in the following areas:
- Education
- Human Services
- Liberal Arts/General Studies
- Marketing/Retailing
- Merchandising
- Native American Studies
- Secretarial Studies
- Office Management

FEES

Cost per academic semester: tuition $1900.

TURTLE MOUNTAIN COMMUNITY COLLEGE

Turtle Mountain Community College is an independent two-year coeducational college, founded in 1972.

THE INSTITUTION

The Address: **Turtle Mountain Community College**
Belcourt, North Dakota 58316
Telephone: (701) 477-5605

The 10-acre site enjoys an enrollment of approximately 500 students.

ACADEMIC PROGRAM

The college offers the Associate of Arts, Associate of Science, and the Associate of Applied Science.

Majors are available in art, biological sciences, business administration, computer science, early childhood education, engineering, English, history, home economics, human services, journalism, liberal arts/general studies, mathematics, medical records, medical technology, natural resource management, nursery, occupational therapy, physical therapy, public administration, science, secretarial studies/office management, social science, social work, and wildlife management.

FEES

Cost: tuition $120.

UNITED TRIBES TECHNICAL COLLEGE

United Tribes Technical College is a federally supported two-year coeducational college, founded in 1969.

THE INSTITUTION

The Address:　　**United Tribes Technical College**
Bismarck, North Dakota 58504
Telephone: (701) 255-3285

The College is a small town campus of 105 acres. The enrollment averages 250 students with housing spaces able to accommodate 146 students.

ACADEMIC PROGRAM

Majors are offered in automotive technology, business administration, child psychology/child development, criminal justice, early childhood education, medical records services and nursing.

FEES

Cost per academic year: tuition and fees $3000, room and board $2500.

Ohio

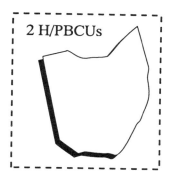

2 H/PBCUs

CENTRAL STATE UNIVERSITY

The University was originally chartered in 1887 as a department of Wilberforce University. The first instruction at the postsecondary level was in 1888. The college became a four-year institution in 1941.

CHRONOLOGY OF NAME CHANGES

1887	-	Combined Normal and Industrial Department of Wilberforce University
1941	-	College of Education and Industrial Arts
1951	-	Central State College
1965	-	Central State University

THE INSTITUTION

The 60-acre campus is located in Wilberforce, Ohio. It is approximately an equal distance from the cities of Cincinnati, and the capitol - Columbus. Dayton (18 miles east of the campus) is the nearest metropolitan area. All modes of transportation are available to the campus and the university's proximity to the large cities makes for a very active environment.

The Address: **Central State University**
1400 Brush Row Road
Wilberforce, Ohio 45384
Telephone: (513) 376-6332

Central State is a coeducational state-supported institution with an average enrollment of 2500 students and a student/faculty ratio of twenty-to-one. On-campus residence halls house 80 percent of the student body.

ACADEMIC PROGRAM

Academically, the institution is divided into four colleges:
- College of Arts and Sciences
- Business Administration
- Education
- University College

The University College monitors the academic progress of the incoming student.

The college offers degrees in:
- Biological Science
- Communications
- Education
- Fine and Applied Arts
- Home Economics
- Physical Sciences
- Public Affairs/Services
- Water Resources Management
- Business and Management
- Computer/Info. Sciences
- Engineering Sciences
- Foreign Language
- Mathematics
- Psychology
- Social Sciences

In addition to traditional degree programs, certificates in African-American studies and interdisciplinary programs in the allied health fields are available.

The dual-degree program in engineering is available with Wright State University. The associate and the bachelor's degrees are offered by the university.

FEES

Cost per academic year: tuition, room and board $8500.

DISTINGUISHED ALUMNI

Leontyne Price	-	Prima Donna
Clay Dixon	-	Mayor, Dayton Ohio
		Elected 1987
John W. Shannon	-	Asst. Secretary of the Army, 1985
Joshua Smith	-	Founder/CEO, The Maxima Corp.
Don H. Barden	-	CEO Barden Cablevision
Dr. Arthur E. Thomas	-	Alumnus, President
		Central State University

WILBERFORCE UNIVERSITY

Wilberforce University is a private institution affiliated with the African Methodist Episcopal Church. It was established in 1843 and issued the first postsecondary instruction in 1856. The first baccalaureate was awarded in 1857. It has the distinction of being the oldest predominantly Black private university in the United States.

CHRONOLOGY OF NAME CHANGES

1843 - Ohio African University
1856 - Wilberforce University of the Methodist Episcopal Church
1863 - Wilberforce University

THE INSTITUTION

Wilberforce is located 20 miles from Dayton, the nearest metropolitan area. It is approximately 65 miles from both Cincinnati (to the southeast) and the capital, Columbus (to the northwest). An airport is less than 30 miles from campus and passenger rail service is 22 miles away.

The Address: **Wilberforce University**
                 Wilberforce, Ohio 45384-1091
                 Telephone: (513) 376-2911

The average enrollment at the college is 800 and the on-campus housing can accommodate 90 percent of the student body. The student/faculty ratio is twenty-to-one.

ACADEMIC PROGRAM

The baccalaureate degree is offered in twenty-one areas including accounting, art/advertising, biology, chemistry, communications, economics, English, finance/banking, health care administration, mathematics, physical science, political science/government, psychology, social welfare work, and sociology. Additionally, the dual-degree program in engineering and computer science is offered in conjunction with the University of Dayton.

FEES

Cost per academic year: tuition $6000, room and board $3200.

DISTINGUISHED ALUMNI

Hattie Q. Brown	-	Founder and President Ohio State Federation of Women and National Association of Colored Women
Floyd Flake	-	1st Full-term African-American Congressman from the 6th Congressional District
Bayard Rustin	-	Activist, Botherhood of Sleeping Car Porters
Orchid I. Johnson	-	Political Activist Founder, Freedom Inc. State Representative, 25th District, Missouri

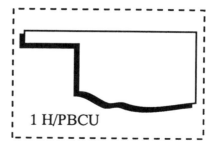

1 H/PBCU

LANGSTON UNIVERSITY

The state-controlled land-grant institution offered its first postsecondary instruction in 1897 and the first baccalaureate was awarded in 1901.

CHRONOLOGY OF NAME CHANGES

1897 - Colored Agricultural and Normal University
1941 - Langston University

THE INSTITUTION

Located 45 miles from Oklahoma City (the state capital and largest city), and 90 miles from Tulsa (the state's largest oil refining center), the university is readily accessible to all forms of transportation.

The Address: **Langston University**
P.O. Box 907
Langston, Oklahoma 73050
Telephone: (405) 466-2231

The students come from 26 states and 18 foreign countries. On-campus housing can accommodate 50 percent of the student body with an additional ten percent in off-campus institutionally- controlled housing. The student/faculty ratio is thirty-to-one. Langston University has 444 acres with an enrollment over 1000 students.

ACADEMIC PROGRAM

The university offers the associate, bachelor's, master's and Ph.D. degrees. The major areas of concentration are agriculture and natural resources, biological sciences, business and management, communication, computer and information sciences, education, engineering, fine and applied arts, health professions, home economics, mathematics, physical education, psychology, public affairs and services, and social services. Graduate study in English as-a-second-language, Bilingual multi-cultural elementary education and urban education is also available.

FEES

Cost per academic year: tuition $4000, room and board $2400.

DISTINGUISHED ALUMNI

Dr. Nathan Hare	-	Chairman, The Black Think Tank San Francisco, CA
Dr. James Abram	-	Department Head, Biology Norfolk State College
Dr. Henry Ponder	-	President, Fisk University
Julia Reed Hare	-	Director, Community Affairs Golden West Broadcasters KSFO
Robert DoQui	-	Entertainer (Movie) Los Angeles, CA

 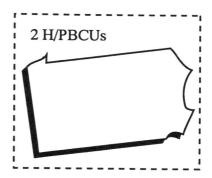

Pennsylvania

2 H/PBCUs

CHEYNEY UNIVERSITY OF PENNSYLVANIA

Cheyney has been described as the oldest historically Black institution of higher learning in the United States. It was originally located in Philadelphia, established there by the Quakers in 1837. The first instruction at the postsecondary level was offered in 1931.

CHRONOLOGY OF NAME CHANGES

1837	-	Cheyney University of Pennsylvania
1842	-	Institute for Colored Youth
1913	-	Cheyney Training School for Teachers
1921	-	State Normal School
1932	-	Cheyney State Teachers College
1959	-	Cheyney State College
1982	-	Cheyney University of Pennsylvania

THE INSTITUTION

Cheyney is located 24 miles west of Philadelphia in suburban Delaware County. The campus is served by a mass transit bus system, while passenger rail service is one mile away and air service is 15 miles from campus.

The Address: **Cheyney University of Pennsylvania**
Cheyney, Pennsylvania 19319
Telephone: (215) 399-2000
1-800-CHEYNEY

The 275-acre campus combines modern and traditional architecture providing an environment that encourages serious studying for the more than 1500 students. On-campus students live in five dormitories which can accommodate fifty-five percent of the student body. This public coeducational school offers opportunity for students to achieve a well-rounded education by combining superior academic programs with rich and varied student activities outside the classroom. Cheyney is part of the 14 Universities run by the Pennsylvania State System of Higher Education.

The college has an athletic program that consists of nine sports. The women's basketball team competes in NCAA Division I level.

ACADEMIC PROGRAM

Cheyney offers the bachelor's degree in accounting, art, biology business, chemistry, communication, computer science, drama, earth science, economics, education, English, geography, health and physical education, history, home economics, hotel/restaurant management, industrial arts, language arts, marine science, mathematics, music, nutrition, police science, political science, psychology, social science, theater arts and urban studies.

Graduate programs offer the Master of Arts, Master of Science and Master of Education. Areas of concentration for the graduate program are elementary education, special education, industrial arts education, secondary education, educational administration, adult and continuing education, general science, foreign language and communication arts. Dual-degree programs are offered with Meharry for medical and biosciences and Pennsylvania College of Podiatry for podiatry.

FEES

Cost per academic year: tuition, room and board $8000.

DISTINGUISHED ALUMNI

Robert Woodson -	President, National Center for Neighborhood Enterprise
Ed Bradley -	Co-host, CBS News Program "60 Minutes"
Martin Ryder -	Director, Secondary Education Program Norfolk State College
Andre Waters -	Pro-football player, Philadelphia Eagles
Marvin Frazier -	Pro-football player, Denver, Broncos
Yolanda Laney & - Valerie Walker	Kodak All-American Basketball players
Rosalyn T. Jones -	Professor, Albany State College

LINCOLN UNIVERSITY (PA)

Lincoln was the first college established in the United States to have, as its original purpose, the higher education of youth of African descent. The university was founded by a Presbyterian Minister and as late as the 1900s, only accepted whites on its faculty. It was established and chartered as Ashmun Institute and offered the first instruction at the postsecondary level in 1854. It was renamed in honor of slain president, Abraham Lincoln. The first baccalaureate was awarded in 1868.

CHRONOLOGY OF NAME CHANGES

1854 - Ashmun Institute
1866 - Lincoln University

THE INSTITUTION

Lincoln University is surrounded by rolling farmlands and wooded hilltops of southern Chester county, Pennsylvania. Philadelphia, the largest metropolitan area, is forty-five miles north of campus. Oxford, the town nearest the campus is four miles south. An airport (90 miles away) and passenger rail service (50 miles away) make access to the campus relatively easy.

The Address: **Lincoln University**
Old Route 1
Lincoln University, Pennsylvania 19532
Telephone: (215) 932-8300

The university has an average enrollment of 1200 students on a campus that occupies 422 acres. The student/faculty ratio is fifteen-to-one. The dormitories, a part of the 27 major buildings, provide on-campus housing for 90 percent of the students.

ACADEMIC PROGRAM

Academic degrees awarded are the associate, bachelor and master degrees. Study abroad programs are available.

Majors are offered in accounting, biology, business, chemistry, computer science, economics, education, English, health and physical education, history, human services, languages, music, philosophy, physics, political science, psychology, public administration, religion, social science, and sociology/anthropology. The Lincoln Advanced Science and Engineering Reinforcement Program (LASER) is recognized as one of the most successful in the nation.

A dual-program in engineering with Drexel University, Lafayette College and Pennsylvania State University, and in international service with American University are among the options available for students.

A special honors program emphasizing attention to global, social issues and the critical languages and cultures—Russian, Chinese, Arabic and Japanese—is available. To participate in this program, students must have SAT scores above 850 and a 3.0 GPA.

FEES

Cost per academic year: tuition $4100, room and board $2700.

DISTINGUISHED ALUMNI

Thurgood Marshall	-	1st African-American United States Supreme Court Justice
Langston Hughes	-	World acclaimed poet
Nnamdi Azikiwe	-	1st President of Nigeria
Roscoe Lee Browne	-	Author/Actor of Stage and Screen
James L. Usry	-	1st African-American Mayor of Atlantic City
Kwame Nkrumah	-	1st Prime Minister and 1st President of Ghana

South Carolina

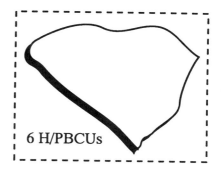

6 H/PBCUs

ALLEN UNIVERSITY

Allen University, the oldest African-American college in South Carolina, was founded in 1870. It is a private church-related school operated by the African Methodist Episcopal Church.

THE INSTITUTION

The University is located in the beautiful city of Columbia, the capital city of South Carolina. All modern means of transportation, air, rail, bus and private car service the area.

The Address: **Allen University**
1530 Harden Street
Columbia, South Carolina 29204
Telephone: (803) 254-4165

The private coeducational institution is situated on 21 acres and has 18 major buildings. Allen has an enrollment of 700 with a student/faculty ratio of eleven-to-one. Five of these buildings have been officially awarded the "Historic District Status" by the U.S. Department of Interior. The University cites as its major objective, to make available for all students, a substantial and organized curriculum in general education. The university lists among its affiliations the American Association of Colleges for Teacher Education, the National Business Education Association and American Association of College Athletic Directors.

ACADEMIC PROGRAM

There are four major academic divisions:
- Education
- Humanities
- Natural Sciences
- Behavioral Sciences

The baccalaureate degree is awarded in the following disciplines: art, biology, business administration, elementary education, English, gerontology, health and physical education, mathematics and music performance, religion/theology, social science, social work and sociology.

FEES

Cost per academic year: tuition, room and board $7000.

DISTINGUISHED ALUMNI

The college has produced ten college presidents, including Dr. W. Dean Goldsby, President, Shorter College, Little Rock, Arkansas.

BENEDICT COLLEGE

Established as Benedict Institute in 1870, the founders of the college were affiliated with the Baptist Church. The college provided the first instruction at the postsecondary level in 1889.

CHRONOLOGY OF NAME CHANGES

    1870 -   Benedict Institute
    1984 -   Benedict College

THE INSTITUTION

Benedict College is located in the heart of South Carolina's capital city, Columbia, and is within walking distance of any place in the downtown area. The city offers a wide variety of leisure activities and historical attractions, a strong support of the arts, as well as quality shopping and dining.

The Address: **Benedict College**
Harden and Blanding Streets
Columbia, South Carolina 29204
Telephone: (803) 253-5120
1-800-868-6598

Benedict is a coeducational private independent college. It occupies 20 acres in Columbia, South Carolina. The 1500 students at Benedict enjoy a student/faculty ratio of seventeen-to-one.

ACADEMIC PROGRAM

The college offers majors in four divisions.
- Division of Business
    Business Administration
    Business Education
    Economics
    Office Automation Systems Management

- Division of Mathematics and Natural Sciences
    Mathematics, Computer Science, Biology, Chemistry
    Physics, Environmental Health Science

- Division of Humanities
    Art, English, Journalism, Music
    Religion and Philosophy

- Division of Social and Behavioral Sciences
    Criminal Justice, Early Childhood Education
    Elementary Education, Community Health, Recreation
    History, Sociology, Social Work, Political Science

Degrees are awarded include the Bachelor of Arts, Bachelor of Science, and the Bachelor of Social Work. A dual-degree in engineering with Georgia Technical and Southern Technical Institute, and in medicine and dentistry with the University of South Carolina is available.

FEES

Cost per academic year: tuition, room and board $7000.

DISTINGUISHED ALUMNI

Dr. Luns C. Richardson   -   President, Morris College
Dr. Jacqueline D. Myers -   Business Professor
                                       Alabama State College

CLAFLIN COLLEGE

Claflin was chartered and offered its first instruction at the postsecondary level in 1869. The private coeducational institution, founded by William and Lee Claflin, is affiliated with the United Methodist Church.

THE INSTITUTION

The college is located about 30 miles from the capital city of Columbia and a short distance from Lake Marion. The twenty-five-acre tract of land is near the business district of Orangeburg.

The Address: **Claflin College**
700 College Avenue
Orangeburg, South Carolina 29115
Telephone: (803) 535-5097

The Claflin campus has approximately 1000 students and a student/faculty ratio of thirteen-to-one. On campus housing is available to the students on a first-come first-served basis.

ACADEMIC PROGRAM

The baccalaureate degree is offered in:
- Pre-Professional Programs
- Pre-Medicine
- Pre-Dentistry
- Pre-Nursing

Degrees are also awarded in art education, biology and biology education, business administration, chemistry, elementary education, engineering tech.,   English, health and physical education, history, management information science, math, math education, mathematics and computer science, and computer science, music, music education, religion and philosophy, and sociology.

The degrees granted are Bachelor of Arts, Bachelor of Science and Bachelor of Science in Education.

FEES

Cost per academic year: tuition, room and board $6500.

DISTINGUISHED ALUMNI

Ernest A. Finney Jr.	-	Assoc. Justice, South Carolina Supreme Court
Jonas P. Kennedy, M.D.	-	Millionaire Turkey Farmer
Bishop Joseph Bethea	-	S.C. Conference of United Methodist Church
Robert L. Alford, Ph.D.	-	Director of Testing Norfolk State University
Mary Honor Wright	-	Educator, established several educational schools in Spartanburg, S.C.

MORRIS COLLEGE

The college was established in 1908 in association with the Baptist Educational and Missionary Convention of South Carolina. It was incorporated and offered first postsecondary level instruction in 1911 and awarded the first baccalaureate degree in 1915.

THE INSTITUTION

The campus is located 30 miles east of Columbia, the capital of South Carolina. The nearest airport is 60 miles from campus and rail service is 40 miles from campus. Bus or car provide easy access to the campus. The town of Sumter has a population of 25,000.

The Address: **Morris College**
North Main Street
Sumter, South Carolina 29150
Telephone: (803) 775-9371

Morris College is a private coeducational church-affiliated institution with an average student enrollment of 700 and a student/faculty ratio of twenty-to-one. On-campus residence halls house seventy-three percent of the students.

ACADEMIC PROGRAM

The college is divided into four divisions:

- Education
- Humanities
- Natural Sciences and Mathematics
- Social Sciences

Majors are available in accounting, allied health, biology, business administration, computer sciences and information, education, English, fine arts, gerontology, history, mathematics, military science, music, religion , social science and sociology.

FEES

Cost per academic year: tuition, room and board $6500.

DISTINGUISHED ALUMNI

Dr. Arthenia Bates Millican	- Former English Professor Southern University
Dr. Ralph W. Canty	- Past President, National Progressive Baptist Convention Member, House of Representatives, S.C. District 66
Dr. Gaosen Tarieton	- Physician, Nashville, TN
James Solomon	- State Commissioner Social Services Department

SOUTH CAROLINA STATE COLLEGE

South Carolina State College is a public coeducational institution founded in 1896.

THE INSTITUTION

South Carolina State is located approximately 60 miles from Charleston and less than 70 miles from the ocean. Students attending the college have access to the beautiful gardens of Charleston and the famed tropical Cypress Gardens. The nearest airport is in the metropolitan city of Charleston.

The Address: **South Carolina State College**
300 College Street N.E.
Orangeburg, South Carolina 29117
Telephone: (803) 536-7000 and 536-7185

Located on 147 acres, the campus has 60 buildings and 12 dormitories which house 60 percent of the 4400 students. The student/faculty ratio is twenty-to-one.

ACADEMIC PROGRAM

The baccalaureate degree is offered in the following areas:

- Bachelor of Arts: art (print making), drama, English, French, history, political science, sociology, Spanish, speech pathology, social studies and music.

- Bachelor of Science: accounting, agri-business, art, biology, business administration, chemistry, computer science, counselor education, criminal justice, economics, education, engineering, foods and nutrition, health education, home economics, industrial education, mathematics, nursing, physical education, physics, psychology, and social welfare, Spanish.

Additionally, the college offers the Master of Arts, Master of Science, Master of Education and Educational Specialist and the Doctor of Education.

FEES

Cost per academic year: tuition, room and board $6000.

DISTINGUISHED ALUMNI

Dr. Emily M. Chapman	-	Administrator, Urban Center Lincoln University (PA)
Eric M. Westbury	-	Asst. President, First Union National Bank of South Carolina
Marianna W. Davis	-	1st Woman to serve on South Carolina Commission on Higher Education
James O. Heyward	-	Director of Admission Alabama A & M University
Veryl Scott, J.D.	-	Business Department Administrator, Norfolk Univ.

VOORHEES COLLEGE

Voorhees College was established in 1897 as a private college affiliated with the Episcopal Church. It was the first historically Black institution of higher learning in South Carolina to achieve full accreditation by the Southern Association of Colleges and Schools. The college was founded by a young African-American woman, Ms. Elizabeth Evelyn Wright who was determined to start a school for Black youth.

CHRONOLOGY OF NAME CHANGES

1897	-	Denmark Industrial School
1902	-	Voorhees Industrial School
1929	-	Voorhees Normal and Industrial School
1947	-	Voorhees School and Junior College
1962	-	Voorhees College

THE INSTITUTION

Voorhees College is located less than two miles east of Denmark, South Carolina, on 350 acres. It is 45 miles south of Columbia, the state capital, which is the nearest metropolitan area. The airport is 50 miles from campus and passenger rail service is two miles from campus.

The Address: **Voorhees College**
Denmark, South Carolina 29042
Telephone: (803) 793-3351

The tree-shaded campus provides on-campus housing for seventy-nine percent of the student enrollment which averages 600. Historic St. Philip's Episcopal Chapel is located on the academic circle of the campus and was built in 1935 entirely by Voorhees students. The student/faculty ratio is fifteen-to-one.

ACADEMIC PROGRAM

Voorhees College offers degree at two levels: associate, baccalaureate and pre-professional programs in Engineering and law. Major concentrations are offered within each of the four academic divisions as follows:

DIVISION OF BUSINESS AND ECONOMICS
- Accounting, business administration, business education, office administration

DIVISION OF EDUCATION AND HUMANITIES
- Elementary education, English education, English communications

DIVISION OF NATURAL SCIENCES, MATHEMATICS, AND COMPUTER SCIENCE
- Biology, chemistry, computer science, mathematics

DIVISION OF SOCIAL SCIENCES
- Criminal justice, sociology, social work, social studies education, political science

FEES

Cost per academic year: tuition, room and board $6000.

DISTINGUISHED ALUMNI

Leonard Spring	-	Vice President, First Union Bank, Charlotte, N.C.
Dr. Prezell Robinson	-	President, St. Augustine's College
Jerry M. Screen	-	Attorney-at-Law

 *South Dakota*

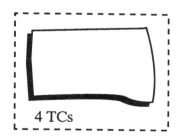

4 TCs

OGLALA LAKOTA COLLEGE

The Oglala Sioux Tribal Council recognized the need for a reservation-based college and authorized planning for such in 1970. In 1971, an institution granting postsecondary degrees and certificates, the Associate of Arts, was established. Today, Oglala Lakota College is a public coeducational four-year college. The Oglala Sioux tribal council's primary mission in establishing the college was to provide academic, tribal, and cultural resources for the Pine Ridge Reservation community.

THE INSTITUTION

The Address: **Oglala Lakota College**
P.O. Box 490
Kyle, South Dakota 57752
Telephone: (605) 455-2321

Oglala Sioux Community College
Pine Ridge, South Dakota 57770

The small college with approximately 1000 students, is located in the southwestern section of the state of South Dakota. The college offers courses in ten regional centers, situated in the main population centers of the 7000 square mile reservation. These centers are in addition to the central campus which includes five buildings spread across the Pine Ridge reservation.

ACADEMIC PROGRAM

Oglala Lakota College is a comprehensive institution offering the Associate and Bachelor degree in a wide range of majors. The college has developed a masters program in tribal leadership and management. The undergraduate programs are in business, teaching and human services. The Associate in Applied Science and the Associate of Arts degrees are offered. The Associate of Arts is primarily for transfer to the four-year program. Degrees are offered in:

- Business
  - Business Administration/Small Business Development
  - Business Administration/Tribal Management

- Education
  - Elementary Education

- Social Science
  - Human Service/Criminal Justice
  - Human Service/Early Childhood
  - Human Service/Social Work and Counseling

- Nursing

- General Studies

- Lakota Studies

FEES

Cost per academic semester: tuition for full-time students $400.

SINTE GLESKA UNIVERSITY

Sinte Gleska University is a four-year institution founded in 1970. It is a private coeducational comprehensive institution located on the Sioux Reservation.

THE INSTITUTION

The Address: **Sinte Gleska University**
                 P.O. Box 490
                 Rosebud, South Dakota 57570-0490
                 Telephone: (605) 747-2263

It is one of the few four-year institutions specifically oriented to and focused upon the education of Native Americans beyond the two-year postsecondary level. The 52-acre campus provides training for approximately 650 students. There is no on-campus housing. Sinte Gleska is primarily a commuter college.

ACADEMIC PROGRAM

The college offers the Associate, the Bachelor and the Master degrees, in a comprehensive array of disciplines.

FEES

Cost per academic semester: tuition $2000.

SISSETON-WAHPETON COMMUNITY COLLEGE

Sisseton-Wahpeton Community College, founded in 1979, is authorized to develop and operate programs granting Associate degrees and Certificates of Achievement. It is a federally-supported two-year coeducational college.

THE INSTITUTION

The Address: **Sisseton-Wahpeton Community College**
Sisseton, South Dakota 57262
Telephone: (605) 698-3966

The 2-acre rural campus os located in South Dakota's southeast corner, less than five miles from the Minnesota border. It provides an academic environment that encourages and supports the maintenance of tribal customs. The campus enrollment is approximately 200 students.

ACADEMIC PROGRAM

The Associate of Arts and the Associate of Science degrees are offered in the following majors:
* Accounting
* Business Administration
* Computer Information System
* Early Childhood Education

- Guidance/Counseling
- Human Services
- Liberal Arts/General Studies
- Native American Studies
- Nursing
- Retail Management
- Secretarial Studies/Office Management
- Social Work

Certificates are awarded in:
- Carpentry
- Electronic Technology
- Plumbing
- Secretarial Studies

FEES

Cost per academic semester: tuition and fees $2600.

Tennessee

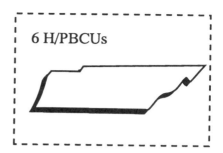

6 H/PBCUs

FISK UNIVERSITY

Fisk University, founded in 1866, is a private coeducational liberal arts institution. The first postsecondary instruction was offered in 1871 and the first baccalaureate degree was awarded in 1875. Fisk was the first historically Black college to gain full accreditation by the Southern Association of Colleges and Schools. It was the first historically Black college to be awarded university status.

CHRONOLOGY OF NAME CHANGES

    1866 -   Fisk School
    1967 -   Fisk University

THE INSTITUTION

Fisk is located two miles from downtown Nashville. Being located in the capital and second largest city in Tennessee, students have access to a part of the rich history of the south. The 46-acre campus has 28 major buildings and is listed in the national historic registry. There are 17 other colleges nearby.

All major forms of transportation are available to the campus.

The Address: **Fisk University**
                1000 17th Avenue, North
                Nashville, Tennessee 37208-3051
                Telephone: (615) 329-8665

The enrollment at the campus averages 800 with a student/faculty ratio of eleven-to-one.

Fisk students may participate in a number of extracurricular activities including the Fisk Jubilee Singers, the Orchesis Dance Club, the Stagecrafters, Greek letter fraternities and sororities, and intramural and intercollegiate athletics.

The library is noted for its special collections such as: The Negro Collection which includes personal papers of Langston Hughes, Marcus Garvey and W.E. B. Dubois; the Black Oral History Collection and the George Gershwin Collection of Music. Additionally, the university has one of the most outstanding art galleries in any southern school with the Steiglitz Collection donated by Georgia O'Keeffe, and paintings of Cezanne and Renoir.

ACADEMIC PROGRAM

The academic program offers liberal arts and pre-professional programs leading to the Bachelor of Arts, Bachelor of Science and Master of Arts degrees. The major departments are:

- Business Administration
- Humanities and Fine Arts
- Natural Sciences and Mathematics
- Social Sciences

Graduate studies are available in:
* Biology
* Business
* Chemistry
* Physics
* Psychology
* Sociology/Gerontology

Pre-Professional Programs:
* Pre Medical
* Pre Dental
* Nursing and Medical Technology
* Pre Law
* Dual Degree in Science and Engineering
* Preparation for the MBA
* Teacher Certification

The following dual-degree or joint programs are offered: science and engineering with Vanderbilt; science and pharmacy with Howard University; elementary education with George Peabody College; nursing and medical technology with Rush-Presbyterian-St. Luke Medical Center in Chicago, Illinois, and the Master of Business Administration with Owen School of Management at Vanderbilt University.

FEES

Cost per academic year: tuition, room and board $8000.

DISTINGUISHED ALUMNI

William Edward Burgharot Du Bois-	Historian, Scholar Educator,
Wilhelmina Delco	- Speaker Pro Tempore State of Texas
John Hope Franklin	- Historian, Educator
Roland Hayes	- Professional Singer

KNOXVILLE COLLEGE

Knoxville is a private college affiliated with the United Presbyterian Church. The college was established in 1863 as a school for Negro youth. The first postsecondary level instruction was offered in 1877 and the first baccalaureate degree was awarded in 1883.

CHRONOLOGY OF NAME CHANGES

    1863 - McKee School for Negro Youth
    1875 - Knoxville College

THE INSTITUTION

Located in the eastern part of Tennessee and close to the Great Smoky Mountain National Park, it is 20 miles north of Oak Ridge, headquarters for Tennessee Valley Authority and the American Museum of Atomic Energy. There is mass transit available, and the city is easily accessible by air or rail transportation.

The Address: **Knoxville College**
901 College Street W
Knoxville, Tennessee 37921
Telephone: (615) 524-6525

The 50-acre campus has an average enrollment of 1300 students. Campus housing is available for fifty-two percent of the student body. The student/faculty ratio is twelve-to-one. Intercollegiate athletics is a part of the activities available to the students.

ACADEMIC PROGRAM

The major areas of concentrations are biological sciences, business and management, communications, education, fine and applied arts, mathematics, psychology and social sciences.

The degrees awarded are Associate of Arts, Bachelor of Arts, and Bachelor of Science.

FEES

Cost per academic year: tuition $4800, room $3400, board $1250.

DISTINGUISHED ALUMNI

Johnnie Ford	- Mayor of Tuskegee, Alabama
Dr. John E. Reinhardt	- U.S. Ambassador to Liberia
Dr. Herman Smith	- Former Chancellor, University of Arkansas in Pine Bluff
Edith Irvy	- 1st African-American to take medical training at Arkansas University
Melvyn L. Burroughs, Ph.D.	- Director of Housing Lincoln University (PA)

LANE COLLEGE

Originally established in 1882 as a high school to teach Colored children, the institute awarded its first baccalaureate degree in 1899. Lane College, named for Bishop Isaac Lane, is a private institution affiliated with the Christian Methodist Episcopal Church.

CHRONOLOGY OF NAME CHANGES

    1882   -   Colored Methodist Episcopal High School
    1883   -   Lane Institute
    1895   -   Lane College

THE INSTITUTION

The college is located in the western part of Tennessee between Memphis, the largest city in the state, and Nashville, the capital and second largest city in the state. A bus system and passenger rail service provide transportation to the campus.

The Address: **Lane College**
                  545 Lane Avenue
                  Jackson, Tennessee 38301
                  Telephone: (901) 424-4600

Lane College is a small fifteen-acre campus with an average enrollment of 600 students. On-campus housing is available for eighty-five percent of the student body. The student/faculty ratio is fifteen-to-one.

ACADEMIC PROGRAM

A dual-degree program in computer science with Jackson State University and in engineering with Tennessee State University is available. The college is divided into five major divisions – Education, General Studies, Humanities, Natural Sciences and Social Sciences. The Bachelor of Arts and the Bachelor of Science degrees are offered in a variety of areas including biological sciences, business and management, chemistry, communication, computer and information sciences, education, English, mathematics, music, physical education and sociology.

FEES

Cost per academic year: tuition $3500, room and board: $3000.

DISTINGUISHED ALUMNI

Otis L. Floyd Jr.	-	President, Tennessee State Univ.
David H. Johnson	-	President, Texas College

LeMOYNE-OWEN COLLEGE

The College was established in 1871 as a private school affiliated with the United Church of Christ and the Tennessee Baptist Convention. The first postsecondary instructions were offered in 1924 and the first baccalaureate degree was awarded in 1932.

CHRONOLOGY OF NAME CHANGES

1871 - LeMoyne Normal and Commercial School
1934 - LeMoyne College
1965 - LeMoyne-Owen College

THE INSTITUTION

LeMoyne-Owen is located in the largest city in Tennessee and provides the students with all the benefits of a large metropolitan city: mass transit bus system, air and passenger rail service, shopping malls, theaters, etc.

The Address: **LeMoyne-Owen College
807 Walker Avenue
Memphis, Tennessee 38126
Telephone: (901) 942-7302**

The fifteen-acre campus has an average enrollment of 1000 students and a student/faculty ratio of twenty-to-one. LeMoyne-Owen is a commuter college. There are no dormitories on campus. The school has a mandatory cooperative education program, offers the dual-degree program in engineering with Christian Brothers College and Tuskegee University, and provides for study abroad in France, Mexico and other countries by individual arrangement.

ACADEMIC PROGRAM

Study programs are available in the following areas: accounting, biological sciences, business and management, computer and information sciences, fine and applied arts, history, humanities, mathematics, natural sciences, occupational therapy, physical therapy, political science, and social sciences.

The institution awards the Bachelor of Arts, Bachelor of Business Administration and the Bachelor of Science.

FEES

Cost per academic year: tuition $4500.

DISTINGUISHED ALUMNI

Benjamin Lawson Hooks J.D. -	Executive Director, NAACP
Marian S. Barry -	Former Mayor Washington, D.C.
Eric C. Lincoln Ph.D LLD -	Consultant, Change Magazine, Professor Duke University

MEHARRY MEDICAL COLLEGE

Founded in 1876 as the Medical Department of Central Tennessee College, the school was reorganized as Walden University and the Medical Department became Meharry Medical College of Walden University. Five years later, the college was established as a separate corporation and has remained so since that time.

CHRONOLOGY OF NAME CHANGES

1876	-	Medical Department of Central Tennessee College
1900	-	Walden University
1905	-	Meharrry Medical College

THE INSTITUTION

Meharry campus is in the northern section of the city, close to two other historically black colleges, Fisk and Tennessee State University.

Transportation in the area is provided by a mass transit bus system, an airport and passenger rail service.

The Address: **Meharry Medical College**
1005 - D. B. Todd Blvd.
Nashville, Tennessee 37208
Telephone: (615) 327-6111

The 62-acre private coeducational institution has an enrollment of 700 students. The student/faculty ratio is six-to-one.

ACADEMIC PROGRAM

The institution is composed of four schools:
* School of Medicine
* School of Dentistry
* School of Graduate Studies
* School of Allied Health

and the George W. Hubbard Hospital.

The graduate degrees awarded are Master of Science, Doctor of Medicine, Doctor of Dental Surgery, and Doctor of Philosophy.

FEES

Cost per academic year: tuition $15,000.

DISTINGUISHED ALUMNI

Alma Rose George, M.D. -	Surgeon and President Medical Staff, Mercy Hospital, Detroit
Robert D. Miller Jr. M.D. -	1984 President, Arkansas State Board of Health
Jacob L. Shirley -	Director, Health Services Albany State College
Marion Perry Bowers -	Member Meharry's Upper Tenth Former Chief Otolaryngology Service, AUS General Hospital Frankfurt, Germany

TENNESSEE STATE UNIVERSITY

Tennessee State was founded in 1912 as a public land grant coeducational institution. In 1979 it merged with the University of Tennessee at Nashville.

CHRONOLOGY OF NAME CHANGES

1912	-	Tennessee Agriculture & Industrial State Normal School for Negroes
1979	-	Tennessee State University

THE INSTITUTION

The College is located in Nashville, the capital and second-largest city in Tennessee. It is served by a mass-transit system, passenger rail service and airport service.

The Address: **Tennessee State University**
3500 Centennial Blvd.
Nashville, Tennessee 37203
Telephone: (615) 320-3741

Tennessee State has an enrollment that averages 8000 and a student/faculty ratio of eighteen-to-one. The main campus has 50 buildings, including dormitories on 515 acres.

During the freshman and sophomore years, all students are enrolled in the University College to complete the general education requirements and to explore career goals before declaring a major.

ACADEMIC PROGRAM

The bachelor degree is offered in the following majors: agriculture, allied arts, allied health fields, animal science, architecture, arts and science, biological   sciences, biology, business administration, chemistry, communications, computer science, counseling/student personnel, criminal justice, dental hygiene, drama, economics, education, engineering, English, foreign language, health care administration, history, home economics, industrial administration/relations, mathematics, medical records administration, music, nursing, physics, political science, psychology, public administration, reading, recreation/leisure, respiration therapy, rural development, sociology and speech pathology and audiology.

The degrees offered are Associate in Applied Science, Bachelor of Science, Bachelor of Science in Nursing, Master of Arts, Master of Arts in Education, Master of Business Administration, Master of Criminal Justice, Master of Engineering, Master of Public Administration, Master of Science, Specialist in Education, Doctor of Education, and Doctor of Philosophy.

FEES

Cost per academic year: tuition, room and board $7000.

DISTINGUISHED ALUMNI

Oprah Winfrey	-	Television Star and Producer
Wilma Rudolph	-	Olympic Gold medalist -Track
Hazo W. Carter, Jr.	-	9th President, West Virginia State
Brenda F. Savage	-	Assoc. Professor, Lincoln Univ. (PA)
Dick Griffey	-	CEO Dick Griffey Productions (CA)

Azie Taylor Morton
Huston-Tilloston College graduate

—First African-American woman
to sign her name to U.S. currency

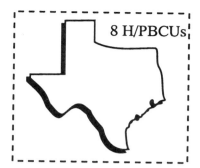

8 H/PBCUs

HUSTON-TILLOTSON COLLEGE

Established as Tillotson Collegiate and Normal Institute in 1875, it was chartered in 1877. The first postsecondary instruction was offered in 1881. The first baccalaureate was awarded in 1909 and it became a four-year college in 1931. The college merged with Samuel Huston College in 1952.

CHRONOLOGY OF NAME CHANGES

    1875 - Tillotson Collegiate and Normal Institute
    1879 - Tillotson College
    1952 - Huston-Tillotson College

THE INSTITUTION

Austin (the location of the campus) was the national capital until Texas became a state. Austin is now the capital city of Texas. The twenty-three-acre campus is served by mass transit bus system, an airport five miles from campus and passenger rail service three miles away.

The Address: **Huston-Tillotson College**
                  1820 East 8th Street
                  Austin, Texas 78702
                  Telephone: (512) 476-7421

Huston-Tillotson is a private coeducational college affiliated with the United Methodist Church and the United Church of Christ. It has an average enrollment of 500 students. On-campus housing can accommodate forty-seven percent of the students.

ACADEMIC PROGRAM

The college is divided into four academic divisions:
- Education
- Humanities
- Natural Sciences
- Social Sciences

Bachelor's degrees have been awarded in the following areas: biological sciences, business management, computer and information sciences, education, mathematics, physical sciences, and social sciences. Intercollegiate sports are offered for men and women.

FEES

Cost per academic year: tuition $4200, room $1000, board $2000

DISTINGUISHED ALUMNI

Honorable Leonard H. Robinson, Jr. -	Deputy Asst. Sec't of State, African Affairs, State Dept.
Azie Taylor Morton -	36th U.S. Treasurer
James Harris -	Nuclear Chemist UC Berkeley
Jesse M. Bethel -	Former Head Mare Island, CA

JARVIS CHRISTIAN COLLEGE

Jarvis Christian is a private liberal arts college affiliated with the Christian Church (Disciples of Christ). The recorded history began in 1904 when Mary Alphin and the Christian Woman's Board of Missions began to plan for a school for Black youth. In 1910, 456 acres of land near Hawkins, Texas, was donated by Major J.J. Jarvis. Initially an elementary school, the school was incorporated as a college in 1928. Senior college courses were introduced in 1937. The first baccalaureate degree was awarded in 1939.

CHRONOLOGY OF NAME CHANGES

    1912 -   Jarvis Christian Institute
    1937 -   Jarvis Christian College

THE INSTITUTION

Jarvis Christian is located one mile east of Hawkins, Texas. The campus is situated in an attractive wooded area of about 1000 acres on US Highway 80. The major industry in the area is the college. Most of the residents of the town are associated with the college. Tyler is 20 miles south of the campus and the nearest metropolitan area is Dallas, 130 miles from campus. Airline service to the Dallas-Fort Worth airport is accessible via Interstate 20.

The Address: **Jarvis Christian College**
U.S. Highway 80
P.O. Box Drawer G
Hawkins, Texas 75765
Telephone: (214) 769-2174

This small coeducational church-related institution of higher education enjoys a student/faculty ratio of ten-to-one. On-campus residence halls house seventy-five percent of the student body, and additional housing is available for married students on a first-come first-served basis.

ACADEMIC PROGRAM

Courses offered are grouped into five divisions and include the following areas:

- DIVISION OF BASIC STUDIES
  Communications
  Humanities and Social Sciences
  Science and Mathematics
- DIVISION OF BUSINESS ADMINISTRATION
- DIVISION OF EDUCATION
  Secondary Education
  Elementary Education
  Physical Education
- DIVISION OF HUMANITIES AND SOCIAL SCIENCE
  Fine Arts
  Literature and Language
  Religion
  Social and Behavioral Science
- DIVISION OF SCIENCE AND MATHEMATICS
  Allied Health and Biology
  Mathematics and Physical Science

Cooperative premedical programs with Fisk University and Meharry Medical College are sponsored by the United Negro College Fund Premedical Summer Program. Semester programs at Brookhaven National Laboratory are available for mathematics and science majors.

FEES

Cost per semester: tuition $4200, room and board $3100.

DISTINGUISHED ALUMNI

Dr. James O. Perpener   -   Alumni who have served as
Dr. E. Wadworth Rand   President of
Dr. C.A. Berry   Jarvis Christian College

PAUL QUINN COLLEGE

The College was founded in 1872 by a small group of African Methodist circuit-riding preachers in Austin, Texas. The college later moved to the city of Waco where it has served the needs of many youth for nearly 120 years. In 1990, the college moved to Dallas and occupies the campus which was previously Bishop College. It is the oldest predominantly Black liberal arts college in the state of Texas.

THE INSTITUTION

The recent move from Waco to Dallas provides students access to one of the most modern cities in America. All modes of transportation are available to the campus.

The Address: **Paul Quinn College**
3837 Simpson Stuart Road
Dallas, Texas 75241
Telephone: (214) 376-1000

Paul Quinn, in cooperation with the Waco Model Cities Community Institute Development Association, established an Ethnic Cultural Center in 1970. The average enrollment at the college is 400 students, with a student/faculty ratio of twelve-to-one.

ACADEMIC PROGRAM

The educational program is organized into four academic division:

- Division of Arts and Sciences
  Biology, mathematics, English, history, political science, language, religion, fine arts

- Division of Professional Studies
    Business administration, office administration,
    computer science, economics, social work, sociology,
    gerontology, psychology, criminal justice

- Division of Education
    Elementary education, secondary education, health,
    physical education and recreation

- Division of Developmental Studies
    Developmental reading, developmental English,
    developmental mathematics

The bachelor degree is offered in: accounting, biology, business administration, computer science, criminal justice, economics, education, English, fine arts, foreign languages, gerontology, history/political science, psychology, social work and sociology.

A parallel-degree program with Texas State Technical Institute (TSTI) makes it possible for students to earn an associate degree from TSTI and a Bachelor of Applied Science from Paul Quinn College. Nine such specialized programs are available.

FEES

Cost per academic semester: tuition $1500, room and board $2500.

DISTINGUISHED ALUMNI

Leon Dorsey - Owner, President Dorsey-Keatts
                Funeral Home, Inc.

PRAIRIE VIEW A & M UNIVERSITY

Prairie View was established as an agricultural school and offered the first instruction at the postsecondary level in 1878. The first baccalaureate degree was awarded in 1902. In 1984, Prarie View University joined the University of Texas at Austin and Texas A & M University.

CHRONOLOGY OF NAME CHANGES

1876 - Alta Vista Agriculture College
1895 - Prairie View Normal and Industrial College
1945 - Prairie View University
1947 - Prairie View Agricultural and Mechanical College of Texas
1971 - Prairie View Agricultural and Mechanical University
1973 - Prairie View A & M University

THE INSTITUTION

The university is situated on a 1440-acre site in Waller County, 40 miles northwest of Houston. It is accessible by major highways and the Houston International Airport. The semi-rural city environment has access to Houston, a major metropolis offering a variety of restaurants, shopping facilities and ethnic festivals.

The Address: **Prairie View A & M University**
P.O. Box 66
Prairie View, Texas 77446-0066
Telephone: 1-800-833-8349

The enrollment at PV averages 5800 with slightly more men than women. On-campus housing consists of nine residence halls capable of accommodating eighty percent of the students.

ACADEMIC PROGRAM

The university offers the following undergraduate degrees: the Bachelor of Arts, Bachelor of Arts in Social Work, Bachelor of Architecture, Bachelor of Business Administration, Bachelor of Music and Bachelor of Science in agriculture, accounting, art, biology, business education, chemical engineering, chemistry, civil engineering, communications, computer engineering technology, dietetics, drama, economics, education, electrical engineering, elementary education, English, geography, health education, history, home economics, industrial education and technology, law enforcement, mathematics, mechanical engineering and technology, mathematics, medical technology, music, nursing, office administration, physical education, physics, political science, Spanish, and speech.

For the truly motivated students, the Benjamin Banneker Honors College provides the opportunity to excel academically in a positive living/learning setting.

FEES

Cost per academic year: tuition $3000, room and board $3000 to $3600.

DISTINGUISHED ALUMNI

Hobart Taylor Jr.	-	Special Counsel to President L.B. Johnson Board of Directors, Aetna Life & Casuality Co.
Jiles P. Daniels	-	Vice President, Student Affairs Prairie View A & M
Percy E. Sutton	-	Retired, Inner City Broadcasting Corp. (NY)

SOUTHWESTERN CHRISTIAN COLLEGE

The college, chartered as a religious, coeducational institution, was founded and sponsored by members of Churches of Christ. It opened in the fall of 1948 with forty-five students in Fort Worth, Texas. In the founding and establishing of Southwestern, those who participated were motivated by a mutual desire to provide for its students' preparation for effective and successful Christian living.

CHRONOLOGY OF NAME CHANGES

    1948 - Southern Bible Institute
    1949 - Southern Christian College

THE INSTITUTION

With a small beginning in Fort Worth, the opportunity to purchase the school property formerly owned by the Texas Military College in Terrell was presented. The Board of Trustees which had planned to maintain the school at the original location, purchased the military school and moved from Fort Worth to Terrell. On the campus stands the first dwelling erected in Terrell. The octagonal shape construction remains today as one of the twenty surviving Round Houses in the nation.

The twenty-five-acre campus has fifteen buildings, an enrollment of approximately 280 students. On campus housing is available and the student/faculty ratio is ten-to-one. The campus is located thirty-two miles east of Dallas, on Highway 80.

The Address: **Southwestern Christian College**
                Terrell, Texas 75160
                Telephone: (214) 524-3341

ACADEMIC PROGRAM

SWCC has an "open-door" admission policy. A developmental program is available to assist students whose high school records and/or college placement scores indicate a need for additional preparation before admission to standard academic courses.

The College is organized around six divisions:
- Division of Bible and Related Studies
- Division of Business
- Division of Developmental Studies
- Division of Humanities
- Division of Physical Education
- Division of Social Sciences

The baccalaureate degree is offered in Bible and Religious education and the associate degree in Liberal Arts. All full-time students must schedule a Bible course.

FEE

Cost estimate per semester: tuition, fees, room and board $3600.

TEXAS COLLEGE

Established in 1894, Texas College offered its first instruction at the postsecondary level in 1895. The private coeducational school is affiliated with the Christian Methodist Episcopal Church.

CHRONOLOGY OF NAME CHANGES

1894 - Texas College
1901 - Phillips University
1912 - Texas College

THE INSTITUTION

The college is located in Tyler, a town of about 100,000 population. Dallas, the largest and closest metropolitan city, is situated less than 100 miles east of the campus. It is served by mass transit bus system and an airport ten miles away.

The Address: **Texas College**
2404 North Grand Avenue
Tyler, Texas 75702
Telephone: (214) 593-8311

The average enrollment is 500 on a 15-acre site. On-campus residence halls can accommodate forty-seven percent of the student body. Housing is available for married students. The student/faculty ratio is fifteen-to-one.

ACADEMIC PROGRAM

Degrees are offered in the following areas: art, biology, business administration, computer science, education, English, history, mathematics, music, physical education, political science, social sciences, social work and sociology.

Course work may be pursued in non-degree subject matter. These fields include: chemistry, drama, economics, French, geography, physics, Spanish, speech, pre-law, pre-medicine and pre-dentistry.

FEES

Cost per academic year: tuition $3200, room and board $2500.

DISTINGUISHED ALUMNI

E. Grace Payne	-	Chairperson, Los Angeles Harbor Commission
Phyllis Buford	-	Administrator, Medgar Evers College
Dr. Jimmy E. Clark	-	President, Texas College

TEXAS SOUTHERN UNIVERSITY

Texas Southern was established as a state institution and offered its first instruction at the postsecondary level in 1947. The first baccalaureate degree was awarded in 1948. The School of Pharmacy was added in 1955, the School of Education in 1971 and the School of Public Affairs in 1974.

CHRONOLOGY OF NAME CHANGES

1947 - Texas State University
1951 - Texas Southern University

THE INSTITUTION

The campus of 130 acres is located in the heart of Houston, the largest city in Texas and the fourth largest city in the United States. Transportation to the campus is provided by mass bus transit system, passenger rail service and the Houston airport.

The Address: **Texas Southern University**
3100 Cleburne Avenue
Houston, Texas 77004-9987
Telephone: (713) 527-7070

Texas Southern University has an average enrollment of 7500 students. Five dormitories provide housing for 11 percent of the student body. Each dormitory is in close proximity to all of the schools and colleges and the student life center. The student/faculty ratio is twenty-five-to-one.

ACADEMIC PROGRAM

There are seven Schools/Colleges comprising the academic program:
- College of Arts and Science
- College of Education
- College of Pharmacy and Health Services

- School of Business
- School of Technology
- Graduate School
- School of Law

The university offers a variety of undergraduate, graduate, and professional degree programs. The basic areas in which degrees may be received are: accounting, administration of justice, airway science, architectural construction technology, art, bilingual education, building construction management, business education, chemistry, child development, computer science, dietetics, drafting and design technology, economics, education, engineering, French, health administration, history, home economics, journalism, mathematics, medical records administration, music, pharmacy, physical education, physics, political science, power and transportation, public administration, respiratory therapy, social work, sociology, Spanish and telecommunication.

The doctorate degree is offered in counselor education, curriculum and instruction, education administration, higher education, urban education, and pharmacy. Professional degree programs are available in accounting, law, pharmacy and social work.

FEES

Cost per academic year: tuition $4800, room $1500, board $1500.

DISTINGUISHED ALUMNI

Barbara C. Jordan, Esq.	- First African-American female elected to the Congress from the South; First African-American female elected to preside over a legislative body.
Craig Washington	- U.S. Representative, 18th District-Houston, Texas

WILEY COLLEGE

Wiley college was founded by Freedmen's Aid Society in 1873. It is a Christian coeducational institution, affiliated with the United Methodist Church, and named for Bishop Issac W. Wiley. Originally, the college was located in two frame buildings south of Marshall, Texas. In 1880, it moved to its present site. Wiley was the first of the Negro colleges west of the Mississippi River to be granted the "A" rating by the Southern Association of Colleges and Secondary Schools.

CHRONOLOGY OF NAME CHANGES

    1873 - Wiley University
    1929 - Wiley College

THE INSTITUTION

The sixty-three-acre campus is home to 700 students. Dallas, the nearest metropolitan area, is approximately 150 miles from the campus. The airport is 40 miles and passenger rail service is two miles from campus.

The Address: **Wiley College**
                   71 Rosborough Springs Road
                   Marshall, Texas 75670
                   Telephone: (214) 938-8341

Wiley College is a church-related liberal arts institution. The preparation of teachers for elementary and secondary schools has been identified as one of the primary objectives of the college. The small college provides housing for 50 percent of the student body.

ACADEMIC PROGRAM

The academic programs are organized into five major areas:

- HUMANITIES
    - Modern Languages
    - Religion and Philosophy
    - Fine Arts
- BUSINESS AND SOCIAL SCIENCE
    - Business and Economics
    - Hotel and Restaurant Management
    - History, Social Science and Political Science
    - Sociology
    - Nursing Home Administration
- EDUCATION AND TEACHER TRAINING
    - Elementary Education
    - Special Education
    - Early Childhood Education
    - Physical Education
- NATURAL SCIENCES AND MATHEMATICS
    - Biology
    - Mathematics
    - Chemistry
    - Computer Science
- BASIC STUDIES
    - General College Requirements

FEES

Cost per academic year: tuition, room and board $6500.

DISTINGUISHED ALUMNI

James Farmer	-	Previous Asst. Secretary, HEW
Dr. Walter S. McAfee	-	Former Rosenwald Fellow in Nuclear Physics, Cornell Univ. Science Advisor, AMDEL-SA Fort Mon Mouth, NJ
Dr. Thomas W. Cole Jr.	-	President, Atlanta University

Virgin Islands

1 H/PBCU

UNIVERSITY OF THE VIRGIN ISLANDS

The University of the Virgin Islands is a land-grant institution which was established in 1962. It offers unique educational opportunities with many programs incorporating material specific to the Caribbean.

THE INSTITUTION

The U.S. Virgin Islands (a U.S. territory located 1100 miles southeast of Miami) is the home of the university. There are two campuses: the main campus on St. Thomas and a smaller campus on St. Croix. The St. Thomas campus, 175 acres, is located three miles west of Charlotte Amalie and overlooks the Caribbean Sea. The St. Croix campus, 125 acres, is located midway between Christiansted and Frederiksted.

The Address: **University of the Virgin Islands**
St. Thomas
U.S. Virgin Islands 00802
Telephone: (809) 776-9200
                    and
University of the Virgin Islands
RR-02 Box 10,000
Kingshill, St. Croix
U.S. Virgin Islands 00851
Telephone: (809) 778-1620

The university is small, with approximately 750 full-time and 1800 part-time students. The low student/faculty ratio of ten-to-one allows individual attention.

ACADEMIC PROGRAM

The Bachelor of Arts, Bachelor of Science and the Associate of Arts degrees are offered.

The opportunity to participate in the Caribbean Research Institute and the Agricultural Experimental Station affords students a unique view of local plants and animals, environmental and health problems, geology, weather and oceanographic patterns specific to the Caribbean.

The university does its best to assure that no one is denied an education because of the expense. Approximately 80 percent of the students at the university receive some form of financial aid. Both federal and institutional programs are available, as well as student loans. Special scholarships are available for students with majors in areas especially needed in the Virgin Islands, such as marine biology.

A program of academic enrichment for high school students who are underachieving and who meet specified federal guidelines is also available at the St. Thomas campus.

FEES

Cost per academic semester: tuition, room and board $8200.

DISTINGUISHED ALUMNI

Reginald I. Hodge - Asst. Vice President, Business & Financial Affairs, University of Virgin Islands

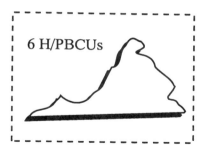

6 H/PBCUs

HAMPTON UNIVERSITY

The Institute was founded in 1868 by Samuel C. Armstrong. Hampton is a private independent institution. The first instruction at the postsecondary level was offered in 1922. The first baccalaureate degree was awarded in 1923 and the graduate program was added in 1928.

CHRONOLOGY OF NAME CHANGES

1868	-	Hampton Normal and Agricultural Institute
1930	-	Hampton Institute
1984	-	Hampton University

THE INSTITUTION

Hampton University is located on the southeast coast of Virginia on the beautiful Chesapeake Bay. Norfolk, ten miles from the campus, is the nearest metropolitan area. The campus is reachable by mass transit bus system, an airport is 13 miles away, and passenger rail service is 8 miles from the campus.

The Address: **Hampton University**
                West Queen Street
                Hampton, Virginia 23668
                Telephone: (804) 727-5000

Hampton is Virginia's only coeducational nondenominational four-year private college. The university, the parent institution, includes Hampton Institute as the undergraduate college, a Graduate College and the College of Continuing Education.

The 47 buildings located on the two-hundred-and-four-acre waterfront campus is home to more than 5700 students, 50 percent of whom are on-campus residents. The student/faculty ratio is eighteen-to-one.

ACADEMIC PROGRAM

The baccalaureate degree is offered at the School of Liberal Arts and Education, School of Business, School of Pure and Applied Science, and the School of Nursing. The master's degree is awarded by the graduate college in biology, business administration, chemistry, communicative science and disorders, computer education, counseling, education, English, environmental science, home economics, mathematics, museum studies, music, nursing, nutrition, physical education, physics and reading. The doctoral degree is awarded in physics.

A dual-degree program is offered in engineering with Old Dominion University. This college's unique offerings include airway science, architecture, radio, T.V. and print journalism, communication disorders and marine science. Additionally, Hampton's nursing program is the oldest continuous baccalaureate nursing program in the State of Virginia.

FEES

Cost per academic year: tuition, room and board $10,130.

DISTINGUISHED ALUMNI

Booker T. Washington	-	Founder of Tuskegee University
John L. Henderson	-	7th President, Wilberforce Univ.
Jerry L. Isaac	-	Asst. to the President Lincoln University (PA)
William Brown Muse, Jr.	-	President, Imperial Savings & Loan Assoc., Martinville, VA
Dr. Sallie Allen-Tucker	-	Assoc. Professor University of Wisconsin
Carl Brooks	-	Vice President, Public Utility Service Corp., N.J.

Hampton University alumni have founded ten institutions.

NORFOLK STATE UNIVERSITY

This state institution was originally established as a junior college and a unit of Virginia Union University. The first instruction at the postsecondary level was offered in 1935. The institution became a 4-year college in 1956.

CHRONOLOGY OF NAME CHANGES

1942	-	Norfolk Polytechnic College
1944	-	Virginia State College
1969	-	Norfolk State College
1979	-	Norfolk State University

THE INSTITUTION

The 102-acre campus is located in Norfolk, the second largest city in Virginia. It is surrounded by Newport News, Portsmouth, Hampton, and Virginia Beach and is less than 20 miles from the North Carolina border, just in the southeast tip of the state on Chesapeake Bay. The mass transit bus system, an airport ten miles away, and passenger rail service 30 miles away provide easy access to and from the campus.

The Address: **Norfolk State University**
2401 Corprew Avenue
Norfolk, Virginia 23504
Telephone: (804) 683-8396

Norfolk State is a public coeducational institution, with an average enrollment of 7400 students and a student/faculty ratio of twenty-to-one. On-campus housing can accommodate twenty-six percent of the student body. Cross-registration is available with Hampton University, Christopher Newport College, Tidewater Community College, Thomas Nelson Community College and Old Dominion University.

ACADEMIC PROGRAM

Majors are available in accounting, audiology, biology, building construction, business education, chemistry, child/family development, computer science/information, drafting/design, economics, education, electronics, engineering, English, fine arts, food science and technology, foreign language, history, hotel and restaurant management, human resources and development, industrial administration/relations, journalism, mathematics, music education, nursing, physical education, physics, political science, reading, speech corrections, trade and industrial technology and urban studies.

FEES

Cost per academic year: tuition $4000, room and board $3500.

DISTINGUISHED ALUMNI

Tim Reid	- Radio/TV Star
James Sweat	- CIAA Coach of the Year, 1991
Karl B. Brockenbrough, CPA	- Senior Account Lincoln Univ. (PA)
Herman E. Valentine	- Chairman and President Systems Management American Corp.

SAINT PAUL'S COLLEGE

Saint Paul's College was established in 1888 in affiliation with the Protestant Episcopal Church. The first instruction at the postsecondary level was in 1922; the first baccalaureate was awarded in 1944.

CHRONOLOGY

1888 - Saint Paul's Normal and Industrial School
1941 - Saint Paul's Polytechnic Institute
1957 - Saint Paul's College

THE INSTITUTION

Saint Paul's is situated near the southeastern border of Virginia, approximately eighteen miles from the North Carolina border. It is slightly more than 60 miles from Richmond, the state capital, to the north and Norfolk and Portsmouth on the east. It enjoys close proximity to the popular resort, Virginia Beach.

The Address: **Saint Paul's College**
406 Windsor Avenue
Lawrenceville, Virginia 23868-1299
Telephone: (804) 848-3111

Saint Paul's College is a private institution with an average enrollment of 800. On-campus residence halls house eighty-five percent of the student body. The student/faculty ratio is thirteen-to-one.

ACADEMIC PROGRAM

The bachelor degree is awarded in the following areas: accounting, biology, business administration, education, English, mathematics, political science, science, social studies, sociology and teacher education.

The degrees awarded include: Bachelor of Arts, Bachelor of Science, Bachelor of Science in Business Administration and Bachelor of Science in Education.

FEES

Cost per academic year: tuition $5000, room and board $3400.

VIRGINIA SEMINARY AND COLLEGE

Virginia Seminary and College is a small private college founded near the end of the 19th century to train youth for Christian service.

THE INSTITUTION

The ten-acre campus is located near the Blue Ridge Parkway, approximately 60 miles east of the West Virginia border and 125 miles east of Richmond, Virginia's state capital.

The Address: **Virginia Seminary and College**
2058 Garfield Avenue
Lynchburg, Virginia 24501
Telephone: (804) 528-5276

ACADEMIC PROGRAM

The major focus of the college program is on Christian education. Degrees offered include the Associate of Arts with majors in liberal arts and business administration; the Bachelor of Religious Education; the Masters of Christian Education and of Divinity. A Certificate in Theology is also available.

FEES

The cost to attend depends upon the number of credit hours of course work selected. The cost per credit hours is $70 at the college and $180. at the seminary. The maximum hours a student may carry varies between sixteen and eighteen. Room and board per semester: $1,300.

DISTINGUISHED ALUMNI

Dr. Ralph Reavis   -   Church Historian, Virginia University
Dr. Noel C. Taylor -   Former Mayor, Roanoke, VA

VIRGINIA STATE UNIVERSITY

The college was established and chartered in 1882. The first instruction at the postsecondary level was offered in 1883 and the first baccalaureate degree was awarded in 1889.

CHRONOLOGY OF NAME CHANGES

1882	-	Virginia Normal and Collegiate Institute
1902	-	Virginia Normal and Industrial Institute
1930	-	Virginia State College for Negroes
1946	-	Virginia State College
1979	-	Virginia State University

THE INSTITUTION

The campus is less than twenty-five miles north of Richmond, the state capital. The largest metropolitan area is Washington, D.C., approximately 135 miles north of the campus. Mass transit busy system, passenger rail service and an airport 30 miles from the campus provide adequate transportation to and from the campus.

The Address: **Virginia State University**
P.O. Box 18
Petersburg, Virginia 23803
Telephone: (804) 524-5902

The enrollment averages 3500 per semester on a campus area of more than 230 acres. On-campus residence halls house forty-eight percent of the student body. The student/faculty ratio is fifteen-to-one.

ACADEMIC PROGRAM

The campus offers cooperative baccalaureate programs in engineering technology and nursing with other Virginia public colleges and universities. The baccalaureate is also offered in accounting, agriculture, animal science, biology, business administration, chemistry, communications, computer science, ecology, education, food technology, foreign language, geology, health and physical education, history, home economics, hotel and restaurant management, international studies, mathematics, music, physics, political science, psychology, public administration, social science, and sociology.

FEES

Cost per academic year: tuition $5000, room and board $4000.

DISTINGUISHED ALUMNI

Reginald F. Lewis, LLB - President/CEO TLC Beatrice Int'l
                                 Holdings, Inc.

W. Clinton Pettus - 1991 NAFEO Distinguished Alumni

Hugh H. Smythe - Former Ambassador to Syria

Gary Dent - Senior Administrator, General
                                 Motors

Artrelle M. Wheatley - Director, Academic Services
                                 University of Virgin Islands

Luther H. Foster - 4th President, Tuskegee University

Mary H. Futrell - Three term President
                                 National Education Assoc. (NEA)

VIRGINIA UNION UNIVERSITY

Virginia Union is a private institute affiliated with the American Baptist Church. It was established in 1865 and offered the first instruction at the postsecondary level that same year. The first baccalaureate was awarded in 1899.

CHRONOLOGY OF NAME CHANGES

1865 - Wayland Academy
1899 - Virginia Union University

THE INSTITUTION

Located in Richmond, the capital city of Virginia, the campus is served by mass transit bus system, an airport less than ten miles away as well as passenger rail service just two miles away.

The Address: **Virginia Union University**
1500 North Lombardy Street
Richmond, VA 23220
Telephone: (804) 257-5881
1-800-368-3227

The university has an average enrollment of 1200 students and on-campus residence halls house sixty-six percent of the student body. The campus area covers 58 acres. The student/faculty ratio is fifteen-to-one.

ACADEMIC PROGRAM

The bachelor's degree is offered in accounting, biology, business administration, chemistry, education, engineering, English history, journalism, mathematics, music, political science, psychology, public administration, religion, social welfare, sociology and theology.

FEES

Cost per academic year: tuition $6500, room $1500, board $2000.

DISTINGUISHED ALUMNI

Lawrence Douglas Wilder -	The nation's highest ranking African-American elected state official and the first elected African-American Governor in the United States.
Adam Clayton Powell Sr. -	Minister, Politician Civil Rights Activist
Benjamin E. Mays, Ph.D. -	Preacher and Educator 1st African-American President of Atlanta's Board of Education
Spottswood W. Robinson III -	U.S. Circuit Judge, District of Columbia Circuit
Charles Spurgeon Johnson -	1st African-American President of Fisk University
Janet Jones -	1986 National President AKA Sorority
Samuel L. Gravely Jr. -	Navy's 1st African-American Admiral
Rondle E. Edwards -	Asst. State Superintendent for Public Instruction, VA Dept. of Education

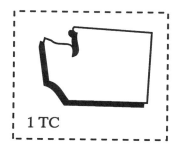

1 TC

NORTHWEST INDIAN COLLEGE

Northwest Indian College is a two-year institution tribally-controlled and chartered by the Lummi Indian Business Council. The college, established in 1978, is funded through the Bureau of Indian Affairs.

THE INSTITUTION

The Address: **Northwest Indian College**
2522 Kwina Road
Bellingham, Washington 98226-9217
Telephone: (206) 676-2772
or 384-8070 or 738-0136

The main campus is on the Lummi reservation in Bellingham, Washington. Off-campus programs operate at Puyallup Tribe and fifteen other reservations in Washington and Oregon.

ACADEMIC PROGRAM

The following degree programs are offered:

* Associate of Arts & Science
College Transfer
Education

- Associate of Science
    - Fisheries Enhancement
- Associate of Technical Arts
    - Business Management
    - Chemical Dependency Studies
    - Civil Engineering Technology
    - Construction Trades
    - Design Engineering Technology
    - Early Childhood Education
    - Fine Arts, NW Indian Coastal Art
    - Human Services
    - Marine Trades
    - Office Professions
- Certificate Programs
    - Business Management
    - Chemical Dependency
    - Civil Engineering Technology
    - Community Health
    - Construction Trades
    - Design Engineering Technology
    - Drafting
    - Early Childhood Education
    - Education Associate
    - Fisheries
    - Marine Trades
    - Northwest Indian Art
    - Office Professions (Office Assistant, Word Processing Specialist)
    - Physical Education/Recreation
    - Surveying

FEES

Cost per credit for residents: $15/credit for 10 to 18 credits for residents

Cost per credit for nonresidents: $40/credit for 10 to 18 credits for residents

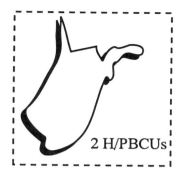

2 H/PBCUs

BLUEFIELD STATE COLLEGE

One of the two historically Black colleges in the state of West Virginia, Bluefield State College was established in 1895. The first instruction at the postsecondary level was offered in 1931. The first baccalaureate degree was awarded in 1932. Though originally one of the historically Black colleges, the population (faculty and students) is currently primarily white.

CHRONOLOGY OF NAME CHANGES

    1895 -   Bluefield Colored Institute
    1931 -   Bluefield State Teachers College
    1943 -   Bluefield State College

THE INSTITUTION

Bluefield is located in the southern most tip of the state of West Virginia, 270 miles from Charleston, the state capital. The campus is about 80 miles from Roanoke, Virginia, and less than 40 miles from the eastern Kentucky boarder.

The Address: **Bluefield State College**
219 Rock Street
Bluefield, West Virginia 24701
Telephone: (304) 327-4000

THE INSTITUTE

The 118-acre site provides a campus area of 45 acres as home to 2900 students. There is no on-campus housing for the state-supported coeducational institution. The college offers the associate degree as well as the bachelor's degree.

ACADEMIC PROGRAM

The College offers the associate and the baccalaureate degree. The Bachelor's is offered in the following areas: accounting, biological science, business and management, computer and information science, criminal justice, education, English, history, mathematics, physical education, physical science, social science, and interdisciplinary studies.

FEES

Cost per academic year: tuition and fees $4000.

DISTINGUISHED ALUMNI

Obie W. O'Neal	-	Dept. Chairperson, Health & Physical Education, Albany State College
Ruth Payne Brown	-	Principal, Baltimore Unified School District
Paul Jonathan Tuffin J.D.	-	Magistrate, Cleveland Municipal Court, (OH)

WEST VIRGINIA STATE COLLEGE

West Virginia State, a land grant college, was charted in 1891 as a school to train Colored people. The first postsecondary level instruction was offered in 1915. The first baccalaureate degree was awarded in 1919. The college has been cited as having produced more generals than any other ROTC department at an historically Black college.

CHRONOLOGY OF NAME CHANGES

1891-	-	West Virginia Colored Institute
1915	-	West Virginia Collegiate Institute
1929	-	West Virginia State College

THE INSTITUTION

Charleston, the state capital and the nearest metropolitan city, is eight miles from campus. A mass transit bus system, an airport 15 miles from campus and passenger rail service ten miles from campus provide access to the campus.

The Address: **West Virginia State College**
Institute, West Virginia 25112
Telephone: (304) 766-3000

West Virginia State College is a coeducational institution with an enrollment that averages 5000 on a 83-acre area. On-campus residence halls house 12 percent of the student body.

ACADEMIC PROGRAM

The bachelor's degree is awarded in art/advertisement, biology, business administration, chemistry, communication, criminal jus-

tice, economics, education, engineering, English, history, industrial arts, mathematics, music education, political science, psychology, rehabilitation services, social welfare, and sociology. The
student/faculty ratio is twenty-to-one.

FEES

Cost per academic year: tuition $4000, room and board $3200.

DISTINGUISHED ALUMNI

Dr. Majorie L. Harris - President, Lewis College of Business
Winston E. Moore - Penologist, Former Director of
Cook County (Ill.) Department of
Corrections
Dr. Morris S. Clark - Oral/Maxillofacial Surgeon
Director, Anesthesia, University
of Colorado, Health Sciences
Joseph E. Turner - Brigadier General
John L. Whitehead - Former President, Tuskegee
Airman Inc., Former Cmdr. Field
Maintenance, Edwards Air Force
Base, Sacramento, CA
Quentin R. Lawson - Executive Vice President
Public Technology Inc., (D.C.)
Dr. Janet Goofrey - First Black, first Female
Headquarters Commander
Kansas Army National Guard
Leander Shaw - Florida State Supreme Court

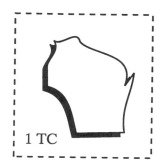

1 TC

LAC COURTE OREILLES OJIBWA
COMMUNITY COLLEGE

The college is an agency of the Lac Courte Oreilles Band of Lake Superior Chippewa Indians. The mission of the Lac Courte Oreilles Ojibwa Community College is to provide, within the Indian community, a system of postsecondary and continuing education with associate degree and certificate granting capabilities.

THE INSTITUTION

The Address: **Lac Courte Oreilles Ojibwa College**
R.R. 2, Box 2357
Hayward, Wisconsin 54843

The college serves approximately 400 full-time students. The majority of the students are from the Lac Courte Oreilles Reservation which is located in the northern lakes and woodlands region of Wisconsin, approximately 150 miles northeast of Minneapolis and 80 miles southeast of Duluth.

ACADEMIC PROGRAM

The college offers curriculum leading to Associate of Arts, Associate of Science, and Associate of Applied Science degrees, one-year certificates, specialized certificates and programs of cultural enrichment. Courses leading to Associate Degrees and Certificates are offered in the following areas:

- Associate of Arts:
     Business (Business Administration, Secretarial Science, Tribal Management)
     General Education
     Health (Alcoholism and Substance Abuse Counseling, Community Health Educator)
     Native American Studies

- Associate of Applied Science
     Paralegal/Tribal Advocate At-Law

- Associate of Science
     Pre-nursing
     Vocational Education
          Carpentry
          Electricity
          Masonry
          Plumbing

- Certificate
     Child Day Care
     Computer Literacy
     Education Aide
     Emergency Medical Services Specialist
     Medical Transcriptionist
     Secretarial Typists

FEES

Cost per academic year: tuition $1200.

APPENDIX A
America's Tribal Colleges & Universities
An Alphabetical Listing with Local Address

Am. Indian Bible College	10020 N. 15th Ave.	Phoenix	AZ 80521
Bay Mills Comm.College	Rte 1, Box 315 A	Brimley	MI 49715
Blackfeet Comm. College	P.O. Box 819	Browning	MT 59417
Cheyenne River C.Coll.	P.O. Box 707	Eagle Butte	SD 57625
Crownpoint Inst. of Tech.	P.O. Box 849	Crownpoint	NM 87313
D-Q University	P.O. Box 409	Davis	CA 95617
Dull Knife Memorial Coll.	P.O. Box 98	Lame Deer	MT 59043
Fond Du Lac Comm. Coll.	2101 14th Street	Cloquet	MN 55720
Fort Belknap Comm. Coll.	P.O. Box 159	Harlem	MT 59526
Fort Berthold Comm. Coll.	P.O. Box 490	New Town	MD 58763
Fort Peck Comm. College	P.O. Box 578	Poplar	MT 59255
Haskell Indian Nations U.	155 Indian Avenue	Lawrence	KS 66046
Inst. of Am. Indian Arts	P.O. Box 20007	Santa Fe	NM 87504
Lac Courte Orielles Ojibwa C.C.	R.R. 2, Box 2357	Hayward	WI 54843
Little Big Horn College	P.O. Box 370	Crow Agency	MT 59022
Little Hoop Comm. Coll.	P.O. Box 269	Fort Totten	ND 58335
Navajo Comm. College	——	Tsaile	AZ 86556
Nebraska Indian C.Coll.	——	Winnebago	NE 68071
Northwest Indian College	2522 Kwina Road	Bellingham	WA 98226
Oglala Lakota College	P.O. Box 490	Kyle	SD 57752
Salish Kootenai College	P.O. Box 117, Hw 93	Pablo	MT 59855
Sinte Gleska University	P.O. Box 490	Rosebud	SD 57570
Sisseton-Wahpeton C.Coll.	——	Sisseton	SD 57262
Standing Rock College	——	Fort Yates	ND 58538
Stone Child College	Box 1082, Rocky Bay Rte.	Box Elder	MT 59521
Turtle Mt. Comm. College	——	Belcourt	ND 58316
United Tribes Tech. College	——	Bismarck	ND 58504

APPENDIX B
America's 4-Year Black Colleges & Universities
An Alphabetical Listing with Local Address

Alabama A & M Univ.	P.O. Box 285	Normal	AL 35762
Alabama State Univ.	915 S. Jackson St.	Montgomery	AL 36195
Albany State College	504 College Dr.	Albany	GA 31705
Alcorn State Univ.	P.O. Box 300	Lorman	MS 39096
Allen University	1530 Harden St.	Columbia	SC 29204
Arkansas Baptist Coll.	1600 Bishop St.	Little Rock	AR 72202
Audrey Cohen College	345 Hudson St.	New York	NY 10014
Barber-Scotia College	145 Cabarrus Ave.	Concord	NC 28025
Benedict College	Harden/Blanding St.	Columbia	SC 29204
Bennett College	900 E. Washington St.	Greensboro	NC 27420
Bethune-Cookman Coll.	640 Second Ave.	Daytona Beach	FL 32015
Bloomfield College	——	Bloomfield	NJ 07003
Bluefield State College	219 Rock St.	Bluefield	WV 24701
Bowie State College	Jericho Park Rd.	Bowie	MD 20715
Central State Univ.	——	Wilberforce	OH 45384
C. Drew U. Of Medicine	120th & Wilmington	Los Angeles	CA 90059
Cheyney Univ. of Penn.	——	Cheyney	PA 19319
Chicago State Univ.	95th St. at King Dr.	Chicago	IL 60528
Claflin College	College Ave. NE	Orangeburg	SC 29115
Clark-Atlanta Univ.	240 J.P. Brawley Dr.	Atlanta	GA 30314
Coppin State College	2500 W. North Ave.	Baltimore	MD 21216
Delaware State College	1200 N.Dupoint Hwy	Dover	DE 19901
Dillard University	2601 Gentilly Blvd.	New Orleans	LA 70122
Edward Waters College	1658 Kings Rd.	Jacksonville	FL 32209
Elizabeth City State Univ.	Parkview Dr.	Elizabeth Cy	NC 27909
Fayetteville State Univ.	Murchinson Rd.	Fayetteville	NC 28301
Fisk University	1000 17th Ave.North	Nashville	TN 37203
Florida A & M Univ.	1500 Wahnish Way	Tallahassee	FL 32307
Florida Memorial College	15800 NW 42nd Ave	Miami	FL 33054
Fort Valley State College	805 State College Dr.	Fort Valley	GA 31030

Grambling State Univ.	P.O. Box 605	Grambling	LA 71245
Hampton University	West Queen St.	Hampton	VA 23668
Harris-Stowe State Coll.	3026 La Clede Ave.	St. Louis	MO 63103
Howard University	2400 Sixth St. NW	Washington	DC 20059
Huston-Tillotson College	1820 E. Eighth St.	Austin	TX 78702
Interdenominational	671 Bechwith St. SW	Atlanta	GA 30314
Jackson State Univ.	1440 J.R. Lynch St.	Jackson	MS 39217
Jarvis Christian College	HY 80 W. Drawer G	Hawkins	TX 75765
Johnson C. Smith Univ.	100-300 Bettiesford Rd.	Charlotte	NC 28216
Kentucky State Univ.	E. Main St.	Frankfort	KY 40601
Knoxville College	901 College St. W	Knoxville	TN 37921
Lane College	545 Lane Ave.	Jackson	TN 38301
Langston University	P.O. Box 907	Langston	OK 73050
LeMoyne-Owen College	807 Walker Ave.	Memphis	TN 38126
Lincoln Univ. (MO)	820 Chestnut St.	Jefferson City	MO 65101
Lincoln Univ. (PA)	Old Route 1	Lincoln Univ.	PA 19532
Livingstone College	701 W. Monroe St.	Salisbury	NC 28144
Martin University	2171 Avondate Pl.	Indianapolis	IN 46305
Marygrove College	8425 W. McNichols Rd.	Detroit	MI 48221
Medgar Evers College	1150 Carroll St.	Brooklyn	NY 11200
Meharry Medical College	1005 D B.Todd Blvd.	Nashville	TN 37208
Miles College	5500 Avenue G	Birmingham	AL 35208
Mississippi Valley St. U.	——	Itta Bena	MS 38941
Morehouse College	830 Western Dr. SW	Atlanta	GA 30314
Morehouse Med. School	720 Westview Dr. SW	Atlanta	GA 30310
Morgan State Univ.	Cold Spring Lane	Baltimore	MD 21239
Morris Brown	643 M.L. King Dr. SW	Atlanta	GA 30314
Morris College	North Main St.	Sumter	SC 29150
Norfolk State Univ.	2401 Corprew Ave.	Norfolk	VA 23504
North Carolina A & T	1601 E. Market St.	Greenboro	NC 27411
North Carolina Central	1801 Fayetteville St.	Durham	NC 27707
Oakwood College	Oakwood Road	Huntsville	AL 35806
Paine College	1235 15th St.	Augusta	GA 30910
Paul Quinn College	3837 Simpson Stuart Rd	Dallas	TX 75241
Philander Smith College	812 W. 13th St.	Little Rock	AR 72203

Prairie View A & M	P.O. Box 66	Prairie View	TX 77445
Rust College	——	Holly Springs	MI 38635
St. Augustine's College	——	Raleigh	NC 27611
Saint Paul's College	406 Windsor Ave.	Lawrenceville	VA 23868
Savannah State College	P.O. Box 20449	Savannah	GA 31404
Selma University	——	Selma	AL 36701
Shaw University	118 E. South St.	Raleigh	NC 27602
Simmons U.. Bible Coll.	1811 Dumesnil St.	Louisville	KY 40210
Sojourner-Douglass	500 N. Caroline St.	Baltimore	MD 21205
South Carolina State	P.O. Box 1568	Orangeburg	SC 29117
Southern Univ.-B.R.	P.O. Box 9614	Baton Rouge	LA 70813
Southern Univ.-Law Sch.	P.O. Box 9614	Baton Rouge	LA 70813
Southern Univ.-N.O.	6400 Press Dr.	New Orleans	LA 70126
Southern Univ.-Shrev.	——	Shreveport	LA 71107
SW Christian College	——	Terrell	TX 75160
Spelman College	350 Spelman Lane	Atlanta	GA 30314
Stillman College	P.O. Box Drawer 1430	Tuscaloosa	AL 35403
Talladega College	627 W. Battle St.	Talladega	AL 35160
Tennessee State Univ.	3500 Centennial Blvd.	Nashville	TN 37203
Texas College	2404 N. Grand Ave.	Tyler	TX 75702
Texas Southern Univ.	3100 Cleburne Ave.	Houston	TX 77004
Tougaloo College	——	Tougaloo	MI 39174
Tuskegee University	——	Tuskegee	AL 36088
Univ. of Arkansas-PB	N. Cedar St.	Pine Bluff	AK 71601
Univ. of Dist. Columbia	4200 Conneticut Ave.	Washington	DC 20008
Univ. of Maryland-E.S.	——	Princess Anne	MD 21853
Univ. of Virgin Islands	St. Thomas	U.S. Virgin Islands	00802
Virginia Seminary	2058 Garfield Ave.	Lynchburg	VA 24501
Virginia State Univ.	——	Petersburg	VA 23803
Virginia Union Univ.	1500 N. Lombardy St.	Richmond	VA 23220
Voorhees College	——	Denmark	SC 29042
West VA State	——	Institute	WV 25112
Wilberforce Univ.	——	Wilberforce	OH 45384
Wiley College	71 Rosborough Sp. Rd.	Marshall	TX 75670
Winston-Salem State U.	601 MLK Jr. Dr.	Winston Salem	NC 27110
Xavier University	7325 Palmentto/Pine	New Orleans	LA 70125

APPENDIX C
America's Tribal Colleges & Universities
By State

ARIZONA
American Indian Bible College
Navajo Community College

CALIFORNIA
D-Q University

KANSAS
Haskell Indian Nations University

MICHIGAN
Bay Mills Community College

MINNESOTA
Fond Du Lac Community College

MONTANA
Blackfeet Community College
Dull Knife Memorial College
Fort Belknap Community College
Fort Peck Community College
Little Big Horn College
Salish Kootenai College
Stone Child College

NEBRASKA
Nebraska Indian Community College

NEW MEXICO
Crownpoint Institute of Technology
Institute of American Indian Arts

NORTH DAKOTA
Fort Berthold Community College
Little Hoop Community College
Standing Rock College
Turtle Mountain Community College
United Tribes Technical College

SOUTH DAKOTA
Cheyenne River Community College
Oglala Lakota College
Sinte Gleska College
Sisseton-Wahpeton Community College

WASHINGTON
Northwest Indian College

WISCONSIN
Lac Courte Oreilles Ojibwa Community College

APPENDIX D

America's 4-Year Black Colleges & Universities
By State & Athletic Association Affiliation

ALABAMA
Alabama Agricultural and Mechanical University[2]
Alabama State University[1]
Miles College
Oakwood College
Selma University
Stillman College[3]
Talladega College[4]
Tuskegee University[2]

ARKANSAS
Arkansas Baptist College[4]
Philander Smith College
University of Arkansas at Pine Bluff[4]

CALIFORNIA
Charles R. Drew University of Medicine and Science

DELAWARE
Delaware State College

DISTRICT OF COLUMBIA
Howard University[1]
University of the District of Columbia[2]

FLORIDA
Bethune-Cookman College
Edward Waters College[4]
Florida Agricultural and Mechanical University[1]
Florida Memorial College

GEORGIA
Albany State College[2]
Clark Atlanta University[2]

Superscripts 1, 2, 3: **National Collegiate Athletic Association Divisions 1, 2 and 3**
Superscript 4: **National Association Intercollegiate Athletics**

GEORGIA cont.
> Fort Valley State College[2]
> Interdenominational Theological Center
> Morehouse College[2]
> Morehouse School of Medicine
> Morris Brown College[2]
> Paine College
> Savannah State College
> Spelman College

ILLINOIS
> Chicago State University[1,4]

INDIANA
> Martin University

KENTUCKY
> Kentucky State University[2,4]
> Simmons Bible College

LOUISIANA
> Dillard University[4]
> Grambling State University[1]
> Southern University - Baton Rouge
> Southern University - New Orleans[3,4]
> Southern University - Shreveport
> Southern University Law Center (SULA)
> Xavier University[4]

MARYLAND
> Bowie State College[2,4]
> Coppin State College
> Morgan State University[2]
> Sojourner-Douglass College
> University of Maryland - Eastern Shore[1]

MICHIGAN
> Marygrove College

Superscripts 1, 2, 3: **National Collegiate Athletic Association Divisions 1, 2 and 3**
Superscript 4: **National Association Intercollegiate Athletics**

MISSISSIPPI
Alcorn State University[1]
Jackson State University[1]
Mississippi Valley State University[1,4]
Rust College[3]
Tougaloo College[3]

MISSOURI
Harris-Stowe State College
Lincoln University[2]

NEW JERSEY
Bloomfield College

NEW YORK
College for Human Services
Medgar Evers College (CUNY)[3]

NORTH CAROLINA
Barber-Scotia College[4]
Bennett College
Elizabeth City State University[2]
Fayetteville State University[2]
Johnson C. Smith University[2]
Livingstone College[2]
North Carolina Agricultural and Technical State University[1]
North Carolina Central University[2]
Saint Augustine's College[2]
Shaw University
Winston-Salem State University[2]

OHIO
Central State University[2]
Wilberforce University

OKLAHOMA
Langston University[4]

PENNSYLVANIA
Cheyney University[1,2]
Lincoln University (PA)[4]

Superscripts 1, 2, 3: National Collegiate Athletic Association Divisions 1, 2 and 3
Superscript 4: National Association Intercollegiate Athletics

SOUTH CAROLINA
Allen University
Benedict College[2]
Claflin College
Morris Colege[4]
South Carolina State College[1]
Voorhees College[4]

TENNESSEE
Fisk University[3]
Knoxville College[3]
Lane College[3]
LeMoyne-Owen College[3,4]
Meharry Medical College
Tennessee State University[1]

TEXAS
Huston-Tillotson College
Jarvis Christian College
Paul Quinn College
Prairie View A & M University[1,4]
Southwestern Christian College
Texas College[4]
Texas Southern University[1]
Wiley College

U.S. VIRGIN ISLANDS
University of the Virgin Islands - St. Thomas & St. Croix

VIRGINIA
Hampton University[2,4]
Norfolk State University[2]
Saint Paul's College[2]
Virginia Seminary and College
Virginia State University[2]
Virginia Union University[2]

WEST VIRGINIA
Bluefield State College[4]
West Virginia State College[4]

**Superscripts 1, 2, 3: National Collegiate Athletic Association
Divisions 1, 2 and 3
Superscript 4: National Association Intercollegiate Athletics**

APPENDIX E
Black Colleges & Universities Supported by the United Negro College Fund

Barber-Scotia College

Benedict College

Bennett College

Bethune-Cookman College

Claflin College

Clark-Atlanta University

Dillard University

Edward Waters College

Fisk University

Florida Memorial College

Huston-Tillotson College

Interdenominational Theological Ctr.

Jarvis Christian College

Johnson C. Smith Unversity

Knoxville College

Lane College

LeMoyne-Owen College

Livingstone College

Miles College

Morehouse College

Morris College

Morris Brown College

Oakwood College

Paine College

Paul Quinn College

Philander Smith College

Rust College

Saint Augustine's College

Saint Paul's College

Shaw University

Spelman College

Stillman College

Talladega College

Texas College

Tougaloo College

Tuskegee University

Virginia Union University

Voorhees College

Wilberforce University

Wiley College

Xavier University

APPENDIX F
Church-Related Black Colleges & Universities

AFRICAN METHODIST EPISCOPAL
    Allen University   (OH)
    Edward Waters College   (FL)
    Morris Brown College   (GA)
    Paul Quinn College   (TX)
    Wilberforce University   (OH)

AFRICAN METHODIST EPISCOPAL ZION
    Livingstone College   (NC)

BAPTIST
    Arkansas Baptist College   (AK)
    Benedict College   (SC)
    Florida Memorial College   (FL)
    Morris College   (SC)
    Selma University   (AL)
    Shaw University   (NC)
    Spelman College   (GA)
    Virginia Union University   (VA)

CHRISTIAN CHURCH (DISCIPLES OF CHRIST)
    Jarvis Christian College   (TX)

CHRISTIAN METHODIST EPISCOPAL
    Lane College   (TN)
    Miles College   (AL)
    Texas College   (TX)

CHURCH OF CHRIST
    Southwestern Christian College   (TX)

INTERDENOMINATIONAL
    Interdenominational Theological Center (GA)

MULTIPLE PROTESTANT DENOMINATIONS
    Dillard University   (LA)

Huston-Tillotson College	(TX)
LeMoyne-Owen College	(TN)
Paine College	(GA)

PRESBYTERIAN, U.S.

Bloomfield College	(NJ)
Stillman College	(AL)

PROTESTANT EPISCOPAL

Saint Augustine's College	(NC)
Saint Paul's College	(VA)
Voorhees College	(SC)

ROMAN CATHOLIC

Marygrove College	(MI)
Xavier University Of Louisiana	(LA)

SEVENTH DAY ADVENTIST

Oakwood College	(AL)

UNITED CHURCH OF CHRIST

Fisk University	(TN)
Talladega College	(AL)
Tougaloo College	(MS)

UNITED METHODIST

Bennett College	(NC)
Bethune-Cookman College	(FL)
Claflin College	(SC)
Clark/Atlanta University	(GA)
Philander Smith College	(AR)
Rust College	(MS)
Wiley College	(TX)

UNITED PRESBYTERIAN, U.S.A.

Johnson C. Smith University	(NC)
Knoxville College	(TN)
Barber-Scotia College	(NC)

APPENDIX G
Scholarships For Undergraduates and Graduates

Most students will need additional funds to cover the increasing cost of obtaining a college education. The following list provides a sampling of scholarships and resources which may be useful in the search for funds to assist in meeting the cost associated with attending college.

Accounting
American Association of CPAs
Minority Scholarships Program
    1211 Avenue of the Americans
    New York City, NY 10036 - 8775
    (212) 575-7641
    NOTE: This $1,000 award is specifically
    for minority students

Scholarship Foundation
National Society of Public Accountants
    1010 N. Fairfax Street
    Alexandria, VA 22314

Architects
American Institute of Architects Foundations
AIA Minority Disadvantage Scholarship Pg.
    1735 New York Avenue N.W.
    Washington D.C. 20006
    NOTE: This scholarship is specifically for
    disadvantaged and minority students

Business
American Business Women's Association
    National Headquarters
    9100 Ward Parkway - P.O. Box 8728
    Kansas City, MO 64114
    (816) 361-6621

Business & Professional Women's Foundation
    2012 Massachusetts Avenue N.W.
    Washington D.C. 20036
    (202) 293-1200
    NOTE: This scholarship awards $1,000 to
    college juniors or seniors.

Y's Men International
    3815 5th Avenue South
    Great Falls, MT 59405

Communication
American Speech-Language-Hearing
Foundation Young Scholars Award for
Minority students
    10801 Rockville Pike
    Rockville, MD 20852
    (301) 897 - 5700

Dentistry
American Association of Women Dentists
    211 East Chicago Avenue
    Chicago, IL 60611

American Fund for Dental Health
    211 E. Chicago Avenue, Suite 1630
    Chicago, IL 60611

Engineers
AGC Education & Research Foundation
    1957 E. Street N. W.
    Washington, DC 20006

Bell Laboratories
Engineering Scholarship Program
    150 JFK Parkway
    Short Hills, NJ 07078

National Action Council for Minorities in
Engineering
    3 West 35th Street
    New York City, NY 10001

National Society of Professional Engineers
2029 K Street N.W.
    Washington D.C. 20006

National Society of Professional Engineers
Educational Foundation
    1420 King Street
    Alexandria, VA 22314

Society of Women Engineers
United Engineering Center
    345 East 47th Street
    New York City, NY 10017
    (212) 705-7855
    NOTE: This $1000 scholarship is renewable.

Fashion
National Home Fashions League, Inc.
    107 World Trade Center
    P.O. Box 58045
    Dallas, TX 75258

Scholarships

Food/Hotel/Restaurant Management
American Dietetic
Association Foundation
450 North Michigan Avenue
Chicago, IL 60611
(312) 280-5000
NOTE: This scholarship is for college students
in their junior year. The award is $1,000.

Club Manager Association of America
7615 Winterberry Place
P.O. Box 34482
Washington D.C. 20034

Diet Center National Scholarship
Diet Center, Inc.
220 South Second West
Roxburg, ID 83440
(205) 356-9381
NOTE:This scholarship is for college students
who are juniors and seniors. The award is $3000.

Hospitality Administration
Educational Foundation of National
Restaurant Association
250 S. Wacker Drive Suite 1400
Chicago, IL 60606-5834
(312) 715 - 1010

Institute of Food Technologist
Junior and Senior Scholarship
Chicago, IL 60601
(312) 782-8424

National Institute for the Foodservice Industry
20 N. Wacker Drive #2620
Chicago, IL 60606

General
American College Scholarship Selection
Committee American Educational Services
419 Lenz Court
Lansing, MI 48917 _no more_

Best Products Scholarships
P.O. Box 297
St. Peter, MN 56082

Business and Professional Women's
Foundation
2012 Massachusetts Avenue N.W.
Washington D.C. 20036
(202) 293-1200

Director, Placement/College Relations
General Motors Building
3044 W.Groud
Detroit, MI 48202
NOTE: This is a full scholarship.

Educational Assistance Ltd.
520 N.Michigan Avenue #301
Chicago, IL 60611

Johnson & Johnson Leadership Awards
1 Johnson & Johnson Plaza
New Brunswick, NJ 08905
(210) 524 - 0400

President's Commission
White House Fellowship Program
The White House
Washington D.C. 20500

State Farm Companies
Foundation Scholarship
One State Farm Plaza
Bloomington, IL 61710
(309) 766-2039
NOTE This is a renewable scholarship and
awards ranges from $2000 - $500.

United Negro College Fund, Inc.
Educational Services Department
500 East 62nd Street
New York City, NY 10021

Washington Crossing Foundation
National Scholarship Award
P.O. Box 1976
Washington Crossing, PA 18977

Journalism/Photography
Gannett Foundation
Journalism Scholarship
Lincoln Tower
Rochester, NY 14604
(716) 262 - 3315

Helen Miller Malloch Scholarship National
Federation of Press Women, Inc.
1105 Main Street
P.O. Box 99
Blue Springs, MO 64015

Scholarships

NABJ (Nat'l Assoc. of Black Journalist)
Scholarships
P.O. Box 17212
Washington, DC 20041

National Newspaper Publishers Assoc.
c/o Louisville Defender
1720 Dixie Highway
Louisville, KY 40210

National Press Photographers Assoc.
Box 1146
Durham, N C 27702
(919) 489 - 3700

Scripps Howard Foundation Scholarship
P.O. Box 5380
Cincinnati, OH 45201

VFW Voice of Democracy Scholar
Broadway at 34th Street
Kansas City, MO 64111
(816) 756 - 3390
NOTE: This award is based on the results of a
national competition and varies from $1,000 -
$18,000.

Medical/Professional
ADHA (Minority Dental Hygienist)
Foundation Scholarship Program
444 N.Michigan #3400
Chicago, IL 60611

American Occupational Therapy Foundation, Inc.
1383 Piccard Drive
Rockville, MD 20850

American Respiratory Therapy Foundation
1720 Regal Row, Suite 112
Dallas, TX 75235

Association of University Programs in Health
Administration
1911 North Fort Myer Drive
Arlington, VA 22209

Commissioned Officer Student Training and
Extern Program (COSTED)
5600 Fishers Lane Rm. 4-35
Rockville, MD 20857

Excalibur Foundation (Physical Therapy)
3430 Baker Street
San Francisco, CA 94123

Excalibur Foundation (Physical Therapy)
3430 Baker Street
San Francisco, CA 94123

ISC Laboratory Technology Scholarship
Committee
818 Olive Street #918
St. Louis, MO 63101

National AMBUCS Scholarships for
Therapists
P.O. Box 5127
High Point, NC 27262

National Health Services Corps Scholarship
(NHSC)
5600 Fishers Lane
Rockville, MD 20857
(800) 638-0824

National League for Nursing
10 Columbus Circle
New York City, NY 10019

Music
Music Assistance Fund
New York Philharmonic
Avery Fisher Hall
Broadway at 65th Street
New York, NY 10023

National Association of Negro Musicians, Inc.
P. O. Box 5-011
Chicago, IL 60628

Physics
The American Physical Society
335 E. 45th Street
New York, NY 10017

Teaching
Paul Douglas Teacher Scholarship Program
Department of Education
400 Maryland Avenue SW
Washington, DC 20202

Phi Delta Kappa Inc.
P. O. Box 789
8th & Union Avenue
Bloomington, IN 47402
(812) 339 -1156
NOTE: (Competitive for high seniors -
essay required)

Links Inc. Scholarship Program
129 St. Paul Street
Brookline, MA 02146

Scholarship Awards Handbook
The Rotary Foundation
1600 Ridge Avenue
Evanston, IL 60201

Soroptimist Federation
1616 Walnut Street
Philadelphia, PA 19103

Soroptimist Youth
Citizenship Award
Contact Local Club

Zonta International
35 East Walker Dr.
Chicago, Il 60601

Church Affiliation
African Methodist Episcopal Church
2311 M Street N.W.
Washington D.C. 20037
(202) 337-3930

African Methodist Episcopal Zion Church
1200 Windermere Drive
Pittsburgh, PA 15218
(412) 242-5842

American Baptist Student Aid Funds
Board of Education Ministries
Valley Forge, PA. 19481

Catholic Negro Fund
Catholic Scholarships
73 Chestnut Street
Springfield, MA 01103
NOTE: This is a renewable scholarship with
awards ranging from $100 - $300.

Coalition of Black Members of the American
Lutheran Church
422 South Sth Street
Minneapolis, MN 55415
(612) 330-3100

Lutheran American Minority Scholarship Fund
Aid Association for Lutherans
4321 N. Ballard Road
Appleton, WI 54919
(414) 734-5/21

Scholarship Aid
Knights of Columbus
P.O. Drawer 1670
New Haven, CT 06507

Student Opportunity Scholarships for Ethnic
Minority Groups
United Presbyterian Church
475 Riverside Drive Rm. 430
New York, NY 10115 or 10027
(212) 870-2618

United Methodist Ethnic Minority Scholar-
ships United Methodist Church
Board of Higher Education
P.O. Box 871
Nashville, TN 37202
(615) 327-2700

The Vocation Agency
National Presbyterian Scholarships
United Presbyterian Church in the USA
475 Riverside Drive Rm. 430
New York City, NY 10115

For the Handicapped
Alexander Graham Bell Associate for the Deaf
3417 Volta Place
Washington D.C. 20007
NOTE This scholarship is for students
majoring in Engineering or Science.The award
is $500.

Chief, Special Services Branch
Division of Student Services
P.O. Box 23772
L'Enfant Plaza Station
Washington D.C. 20026-3772

National Federation for the Blind
RFD #2 West
Willington, CT 06279
NOTE: This $1200 scholarship requires a 250
word statement on how and why it will help.

National Federation of the Blind
814 Fourth Avenue, Suite 200
Grinnell, IA
(515) 236-3366
NOTE: This scholarship award ranges from
$1,800 - $4,000.

Scholarships

Stanley E. Jackson Scholarship
Foundation for Exceptional Children
1920 Association Drive
Reston, VA 22091

Sororities/Fraternities
Alpha Kappa Alpha Sorority, Inc.
5211 South Greenwood Avenue
Chicago, 60615
(312) 684-1282

Alpha Phi Alpha Fraternity, Inc.
4432 South MLK Drive
Chicago, IL 60653
(312) 373-1819

Delta Sigma Theta Sorority, Inc.
1707 New Hampshire Avenue N.W.
Washington D.C. 20009
(202) 483-5460

Iota Phi Lambda Sorority, Inc.
5313 Halter Lane
Norfolk, VA 23502

Kappa Alpha Psi Fraternity, Inc.
2320 North Broad Street
Philadelphia, PA 19132
(215) 228-7184

Omega Psi Phi Fraternity, Inc.
2714 Georgia Avenue N.W.
Washington D.C. 20001

Phi Beta Sigma Fraternity, Inc.
1327 R. Street N.W.
Washington D.C. 20011

Executive Director
Phi Chi Theta Foundation
3703 Washington Blvd.
Indianapol#s, IN 46205

Phi Delta Kappa
P.O. Box 789
Bloomington, IN 47402

Sigma Gamma Rho Sorority, Inc.
840 E. 87th Street
Chicago, IL 60619
(312) 873-9000

Zeta Delta Phi Sorority, Inc.
P.O. Box 157
Bronx, NY 10469
(212) 407-8288

Zeta Phi Beta Sorority, Inc.
1734 New Hampshire Avenue N.W.
Washington D.C. 20009
(202) 387-3103
NOTE: This scholarship awards $2,500.

Scholarships based upon Academic Scores
Harry S. Truman Scholarship Foundation
712 Jackson Place N.W.
Washington D.C. 20006

National Merit Scholarship Corporation
One American Plaza
Evanston, 60201

Scholastic Photography Awards
50 W. 44th Street
New York City, NY 10036

Stanley E. Jackson Scholarship for the Gifted
Foundation for Exceptional Children
1920 Association Drive
Reston, VA 22091
(703) 620-1054

Westinghouse Science Scholarships Science
Service
1719 N.Street N.W.
Washington D.C. 20036

William Randolph Hearst Foundation
690 Market Street., Suite 502
San Francisco, CA 94104
NOTE:Sponsors US Senate Youth Program
available to elected high school class officers.

Scholarships identified especially for Minority Students
Agnes Jones Johnson
Undergraduate Scholarship
Director of Education - NAACP
186 Remsen Street
Brooklyn, NY 11201

DuPont Minority Scholarship Program
Human Resources
1007 Market Street
Wilmington, Deleware 19898
(302) 774-6116

Eastman Kodak Co.
   343 State Street
   Rochester, NY 14650

George E. Johnson
   8522 South Lafayette Avenue
   Chicago, IL 60620

Hallie Q. Brown Scholarship Fund
National Association of Colored Women Clubs
   5808 16th N.W.
   Washington, D.C. 20011
   (202) 726-2044

Jackie Robinson Foundation
Education & Leadership Development Pg.
   80 Eighth Avenue
   New York, NY 10011

National Legal Defense & Educational Fund
Herbert Lehman Educational Fund
   10 Columbus Circle, Suite 2030
   New York, NY 10019

National Merit Scholarship Corp.
   One American Plaza
   Evanston, IL 60201

National Scholarship Service & Fund for
Negro Students
   563 - 3rd Street
   Brooklyn, NY 11215

Newspaper Fund
   P.O. Box 300
   Princeton, NJ 08540
   NOTE: This scholarhip is for college juniors
   and seniors.

Research Fellowship Program
The Rockefeller Foundation
   1133 Avenueof the Americas
   New York, NY 10036

Roy Wilkins Educational Scholarship
   1790 Broadway
   New York, NY 10019

Smithsonian Institution
Office of Fellowships and Grants
   Washington, D.C. 20860

Financial Assistance to Dependent Children
Alcoa Foundation
   1501 Alcoa Bidg.
   Mellon Square
   Pillburo, PA 15219
   (412)553-4786

American Legion
   Contact Regional Leaders

American Postal Workers Union Scholarship
Program
   817 14th Street, N.W.
   Washington D.C. 20005

Army Emergency Relief Program
   200 Stovall Street
   Alexandria, VA 22332
   NOTE: Provides financial assistance to
   children of army personnel on active duty who
   have died or are disabled due to military service.

Avon Scholarship Program
   9th West 57th Street
   New York City, NY 10019

Citizens' Scholarship Foundation of America, Inc.
Burger King Crew Member Scholarship Prg.
   P. 0. Box 297
   St.Peter, MN 56082
   NOTE: This scholarship is for employees of
   Burger King.

Citizens' Scholarship Foundation of America, Inc.
General Mills Scholarship Program
   P.O. Box 297
   St.Peter, MN 56082
   NOTE: This scholarship is to assist dependent
   children of employees of Pillsbury Company.

H&R Block Foundation Scholarship Program
   4410 Main Street
   Kansas City, MO 64111

McDonald's
   McDonald's Plaza
   1100 W. 22nd Street
   Oak Brook, IL 60521
   NOTE: This Scholarship is for McDonald's
   employees.

Scholarships

McDonnell Douglas Scholarship
3855 Lakewood Blvd. M.C 18-47
Long Beach, Ca 90846
(310) 593-2612

Naval Military Personnel Command
Dependent's Scholarship Program
Department of the Navy
Washington D.C. 20370-5121
NOTE: Scholarship assistance to the
dependent children of Navy, Marine and Coast
Guard Personnel.

Navy Relief Society
801 North Randolph Street, Suite 1228
Arlington, VA 22203-1989
NOTE: Provides assistance to unmarried
dependent children of service members
deceased while on active duty.

Oscar Mayer Food Corp.
P.O. Box 7188
Modesa, WI 53707
(608) 241-3311

Rockwell International
College Scholarship
2230 East Imperial Highway
El Segundo, CA 90245
(310) 647-5000

Union Privilege AFL-CIO
Scholarship Program
1444 I Street N.W.
Washington D.C. 20005

Westinghouse Electric Corporation
Families Scholarship Program
Ardmore Blvd. & Brinton Road
Pittsburgh, PA 15221
(412) 247-7222
NOTE: This scholarship award ranges from
$2,000 - $10,000.

Women Marines Association
Scholarship Chairman
282 San Dimas Avenue
Oceanside, Ca 92056

Loan Funds
American Association of Women Dentist
95 West Broadway
Salem, New Jersey 08079

American Baptist Student Aid Funds
Board of Ministries
Valley Forge, PA 19481

BPW Loan Fund for Women in Engineering
Studies, BPW Foundation
2012 Massachusetts Avenue, NW
Washington, DC 20036

Dairy Remembrance Fund
6425 Executive Blvd.
Rockville, MD 20852

Hattie M. Strong Foundation
1625 Eye Street N.W. Suite 409
Washington, DC 20006

Pickett & Hatcher Educational Fund
P. 0. Box 8169
Columbus, GA 31908

Retired Officers Association Scholarship
Loan Program Administrator, TROA
Scholarship Loan Program
201 North Washington St.
Alexandria, VA 22314

United Methodist Church
(Student Loan Fund)
P. 0. Box 871
Nashville, TN 37202
(615) 327 -2700

SCHOLARSHIPS FOR GRADUATE STUDENTS

Publications and organizations that provide
scholarship information free to individual
scholars:

American Association for Gifted Children
15 Gramercy Park
New York City, NY 10003

APSA Graduate Fellowship
American Political Science Assoc.
1527 N. Hampshire Avenue, N.W.
Washington, DC 20030

AT&T Bell Laboratories
101 Crawford Corner Road
P. 0. Box 3030
Holmdel, NJ 07733

Scholarships

Council for International Exchange of
Scholarships
 11 DuPont Circle
 Washington DC 20036

Fellowships and Grants
American Council of Learned Society
 228 East 45th Street
 New York City, NY 10017-3398

Fellowships
John Simon Guggenheim Memorial Fnd.
 90 Park Avenue
 New York City, NY 10026

Flemmie P. Kittrell Fellowships
American Home Economics Assoc. Fnd.
 1555 King Street
 Alexandria, VA 22314

Fullbright and Other Grants for Graduate
Study Abroad
Institute of International Education
 809 United Nations Plaza
 New York City, NY 10027

Grant Guidelines
New York Council for the Humanities
 33 West 42nd Street
 New York City, NY 10036

Hughes Fellowship
Technical Education Center
 P. 0. Box 80028 (C 1/B168)
 Los Angeles, CA 90080

Jacob Javits Fellowship Program
Department of Education
Graduate Programs Branch
 400 Maryland Avenue S.W.
 Washington DC 20202

MBA Scholarships
National Black MBA Assoc. Inc.
 180 N. Michigan Avenue
 Chicago, IL 60601

Minority Fellowship Program
American Sociological Association
 1722 N. Street N.W.
 Washington DC 20036

National Research Council
 2101 Constitution Avenue NW
 Washington, DC 20418

Nurses' Education Funds, Inc.
 333 W 57th Street
 New York, NY 10019

Office of Postsecondary Education
Graduate Program Branch
 US Department of Education
 Washington DC 20202

Overview of Endowment Programs National
Endowment for the Humanities
 1100 Pennsylvania Avenue NW
 Washington DC 20506

Scholarships Guide AFL-CIO
Pamphlet Division
 815 Sixteenth Street NW
 Washington DC 20006

Social Science Research Fellowship and
Grants for Research Social Science Research
Council
 605 Third Avenue
 New York City, NY 10158

Woodrow Wilson National Fellowship Fnd.
 P.O. Box 642
 Princeton, NJ 08542

W. K. Kellogg Foundation
National Fellowship Program
 400 North Avenue
 Battle Creek, MI 49016

Edward A Mellinger Educational Foundation
 1025 East Broadway
 Monmouth, Il 61462

Georgia Harkness Scholarship Award
Program Division of Ordained Ministry
The United Methodist Church
 P.0. Box 871
 Nashville, TN 37202
 (615) 327-2700
 NOTE: Must have an undergraduate degree and
 be a candidate for the ordained ministry.

Black Americans Information Directory. Gale Research Inc. Detroit, MI.

Black Student's Guide to Scholarships. Beckham House Publishers, Silver Springs, MD.

Cassidy, D.J. and Arlen, M.J. *The Scholarship Book.* Prentice Hall, Inc., Englewood Cliffs, NJ.

Chance To Go To College (A). Publications Order Office, College Entrance Examination Board, Princeton, NJ.

Choosing To Succeed. General Foods Corp. Kankakee, IL.

College Blue Book (The) Scholarships, Fellowships, Grants and Loans. MacMillan Publishing Co., New York, NY.

DeGroyter, W. *American Universities and Colleges.* Hawthorne, NY.

Dilts, S.W. *Peterson's Four-Year Colleges.* Princeton, New Jersey.

Directory of Biomedical and Health Care Grants. The Oryx Press, Phoenix, AZ.

Ebony. Johnson Publications Annual August Issue, Chicago, IL.

Financial Aid for College Students: Undergraduate. Government Printing Office, Washington, D.C.

Bibliography

Financial Assistance for College Students. American Council on Educational Studies, Washington, D.C.

Fiske, E. B. *The Fiske Guide to Colleges.* Random House, Inc., New York, NY.

Garrett, R. *Famous First Facts About Negroes.* 1972.

Handbook Of College Financial Aid. Barron's, Woodbury, NY.

Higher Education Directory. Higher Education Publication, Inc., Fall Church, VA.

How To Finance A College Education. Holt and Co., New York, NY.

How To Get Money to Pay for College. McKay Books, New York, NY.

How To Obtain Money For College. ARCO, New York, NY.

Institutional and Presidential Profiles. National Association for Equal Opportunities in Higher Education. Black Higher Education Center. Washington, D.C.

Institutional and Professional Profiles. National Association for Equal Opportunities in Higher Education. Black Higher Education Center. Washington, D.C.

Kesslar, O. *Financial Aid for Higher Education: A Catalog for Undergraduates.* W.C. Brown & Co., Dubuque, IA.

Kohl, K. A. and Kohl, I. *Financing College Education.* Harper and Row, New York, NY.

Bibliography

Lever, W. E. *How To Obtain Money For College.* ARCO Publishing Co., Inc., New York, NY.

Meeting College Costs. College Entrance Examination Board, Princeton, NJ.

National Scholarship Research Service. San Rafael, CA.

New American Guide to Scholarships, Fellowships and Loans. Signet Key Books, New York, NY.

Ploski, H. A. and Williams, J. *The Negro Almanac.* Gale Research Inc., Detroit, MI. 1989.

Profiles of American Colleges. Barron's Educational Series Inc., New York, NY.

Scholarships, Fellowships and Loans. Belman Publishing Co., Cambridge, MA.

Songe, A.H. *American Universities and Colleges: Dictionary of Name Changes.* Scarecrow Press, Inc., Metchen, NY.

Straughn II, C. T. and Straughn, B. L. *Lovejoy's College Guide. 50th Edition.* Prentice Hall, N.Y. 1991.

Student Financial Aid Manual. US Publication, Washington D.C.

Who's Who Among Black Americans. 7th Edition. Gale Research Inc., Detroit, MI.

You Can Win A Scholarship. Barron's Educational Series, Inc., Woodbury, NY.

Index

Index

NOTES

NOTES

·ORDER FORM

America's Black & Tribal Colleges

PLEASE SUPPORT YOUR LOCAL BOOKSTORE!

We at Sandcastle Publishing and Distribution are committed to supporting local bookstores. If you wish, you may write or fax your order directly to us and we will be pleased to assist you.

POSTAL ORDERS: Sandcastle Publishing & Disbribution Customer Service—Order Dept., P.O. Box 3070-A, South Pasadena, CA 91031-6070

PHONE/FAX MASTERCARD/VISA ORDERS: (800) 891-4204

Please fill out form and have your card # and expiration date available.

DISTRIBUTION TO THE BOOKTRADE: (213) 255-3616

Competitive discount schedule, terms & conditions. Will work from store purchase orders. STOP orders OK. If CA business, resale number must accompany order.

Please send the following books. I understand that I may return any books in unmarked and resalable condition for a full refund—for any reason, no questions asked within 7 days of receipt of the book.

Number of Books Ordered: _____ Cost of Books: $19.95 x _____ = _____

Sales Tax: = _____
Please add 8.25% sales tax for books shipped to a California
address. ($1.65 for one book, $3.30 for two, etc.)
Packaging/Shipping: $3.75 for first book plus $1.05/add'l book   = _____
TOTAL   = _____

Please send my order to:

Name _____

Address _____

City _____ State _____ Zip Code _____

Daytime Phone Number with area code first _____